prayerfulness

Awakening to the Fullness of Life

D1316859

Reviews of related books by Robert J. Wicks

Bounce: Living the Resilient Life (Oxford, 2009)
Bounce entreats us to "Have a Life!"—and live it more fully. Wicks helps us to develop hardiness, learn to debrief ourselves after a hard day, and create a personal self-care program we will actually follow. Insightful, practical, and often humorous, *Bounce* is the right tonic for the spirit we need in today's stressful world.

Helen Prejean
Author of *Dead Man Walking*

Crossing the Desert (Sorin, 2007)
Only after the desert has done its work in us can an angel come to strengthen us. *Crossing the Desert* tells us why we need the desert in our lives and what kind of angels only the desert can bring. This is Robert Wicks at his best: wonderfully sane, balanced, accessible, witty, and challenging. Mysticism for those who are frightened of that term.

Ronald Rolheiser, O.M.I.
Author of *The Holy Longing*

Riding the Dragon (Sorin, 2003)
Like a good friend's support in tough times, *Riding the Dragon* is compassionate and wise.

Jack Kornfield
Author of *A Path with Heart*

Everyday Simplicity (Sorin, 2000)
Practical, easy to use, and with profound wisdom and a gentle unassuming manner, *Everyday Simplicity* can help you get started on a spiritual life and sustain it for the long haul.

William A. Barry, S.J.
Author of *Finding God in All Things*

prayerfulness

Awakening to the Fullness of Life

Robert J. Wicks

Author of *Riding the Dragon*

SORIN BOOKS Notre Dame, Indiana

www.sorinbooks.com

ISBN-10 1-933495-30-8   ISBN-13 978-1-933495-30-9

Cover image © Veer Incorporated.

Cover and text design by John R. Carson.

Printed and bound in the United States of America.

Library of Congress Cataloging-in-Publication Data
    Wicks, Robert J.
    Prayerfulness : awakening to the fullness of life / Robert J. Wicks.
    p. cm.
    ISBN-13: 978-1-933495-20-0
    ISBN-10: 1-933495-20-0
    1. Prayer--Christianity. 2. Spiritual life--Christianity. I. Title.
    BV210.3.W486 2009
    248.3'2--dc22

                                                            2009015327

Someone once advised: only marry someone whom you like better than yourself. Over forty years ago, I took this wisdom to heart when I married Michaele Barry. Over these many years, when I have been intense, she has been a calming influence. When I have had doubts, she has had enough faith for the both of us. And, when I have been really lost, she has searched with me until I was able to find myself again. The result? More joy and peace than I deserve. So, it is true. I am living proof of it—you should marry someone you like better than yourself! And so, I happily dedicate this book on the beautiful topic of prayerfulness to someone equally beautiful.

With love, for my wife,
Michaele Barry Wicks

Prayerfulness: Being in the present with your eyes wide open to experiencing God and life in dynamic new ways.

(Synonym: *Spiritual Mindfulness/Awareness*)

Contents

Foreword

P rayer has long been a vital interest of mine. I've stopped counting the years since a desire to experience the Holy One first awakened in me. Suffice it to say that I now gather those many years by decades. In spite of continuous reading and study, daily meditation, and faithful attention to the inner and outer components of my existence, I often feel like a neophyte when it comes to "the spiritual life." There is so much more to learn and relearn. There is always a need for further awakening and an ever greater acceptance of the mystery that weaves through the deeper part of who I am.

Robert Wicks points this out clearly when he notes, "True prayerfulness is not captured once and for all but must be continually embraced." How cognizant he is of both old-timers and newcomers to the spiritual life, of all of us who need to be constantly inspired, nurtured, and offered practical help in order to increasingly embrace prayerfulness.

If you hear Dr. Wicks at a conference, you experience a marvelous combination of high energy, quick wit, skilled storytelling, and valuable insight. When you read his publications, you discover that his thought reflects someone well-versed in both psychology and spirituality. He brings a depth of wisdom and a sturdy commitment to what is of greatest value. All of these gifts shine through *Prayerfulness*.

Robert Wicks brings his best to a topic that has been perused by countless authors. What makes *Prayerfulness* stand out is his unfailing honesty and his ability to unite our everyday life to our relationship with the divine. Dr. Wicks not only presents a solid foundation for the spiritual life but also gives numerous helpful suggestions for how to grow in "experiencing God and life in dynamic new ways." He does so with an engaging manner, assuring us that we are quite capable of attaining what he proposes.

One cannot help but recognize both depth and practicality in the list of characteristics that Robert Wicks considers to be essential to prayerfulness. His list contains equal amounts of inspiration and challenge. This author is not pushy or preachy. His writing reflects the openness that he suggests as essential for prayerfulness. Yet, he is also firm about what is required in order to have an authentic, spiritually focused life.

One of these necessities is that of paying attention to our spiritual blinders, those personality traits that bushwhack us at such times when we are overly busy, caught in a darkness of mind or heart, unaware, or nonreceptive. Dr. Wicks insists that true prayerfulness requires a change in attitude and a deliberate choice to act with love. He reminds us that we cannot avoid the tough issues that haunt most of us: the suffering and difficult times, the questions, doubts, addictions, and concerns that often attach themselves to us. With gentle nudges, he reminds the reader that only by facing and befriending these aspects of our lives will we grow in prayerfulness.

One of the many features I appreciate about Robert Wicks's published works is his sense of humor. He gives his reader an opportunity to see the contradictions and foolishness that keep us from prayerfulness, and he does so without creating a playpen spirituality. While he keeps the reader focused on the seriousness of the issue, his witty phrases and stories enable one to not feel overwhelmed by the truth of what he presents. For example, Dr. Wicks describes those whose life gets overly cluttered or addictively stimulated with activity as people who "rush around like a gargoyle on roller skates." I could easily have fallen back into my old discouragements, remembering a history of feeling inundated with activity, of succumbing to poor-me-isms and irrational frustration due to my struggle with inner and outer balance. Instead, I chuckled at his description, smiling to myself, "Been there, done that." (There are certain places in this book where I also thought, "Still doing that!")

We never completely outgrow what keeps us from entering fully into prayerfulness, but we can get much better at recognizing which parts of us lead us away and which parts draw us closer. Thanks to the guidance of *Prayerfulness*, readers will be better able to move in a direction that orients them toward spiritual maturity.

I always feel safe among the pages of Robert Wicks's writings. He is grounded in healthy spirituality and writes about what he has lived. He also allows us to listen in on what others have experienced and shared with him, so we know we are not alone in our hopes and struggles. He never underestimates his reader's desire to draw more closely to the divine. At the same time, Dr. Wicks wisely cautions: "Take care of yourselves." I like that. His advice leaves me with the conviction that this author not only teaches well, but does so with a compassionate heart.

—Joyce Rupp

Acknowledgments

Stories are at the heart of any book of spiritual lessons. But for there to be stories, there must be storytellers. Among the ones represented in this book who were willing to share their stories to help make other people's stories bigger were: Lorrette Ayers, Cynthia Bourret, Therese Connolly, John Donahue, Barry Estadt, Kim Fauth, Kristen Franks, Marie Gipprich, Joe Healey, Agnes Hughes, Pamela Lowe, Joe Luca, Brianna Luna, Setefano Mataele, Michelle Mesen, Kayliz Oakes, John O'Connor, and Mary Beth Wordel.

I am grateful as well to Mary Catherine Bunting, whose faithful encouragement and belief in my work has made all the difference. Thank you, Mary Catherine.

As always, Bob Hamma, the editorial director of Sorin Books, did his best so what I wrote turned out to be the best I could do.

The ultimate editorial arbitrator for me, who deserves the most profound words of gratitude, is my wife Michaele Barry Wicks. What would I do without her?

I would also like to thank my colleagues in the Pastoral Counseling Department at Loyola University, Maryland, for their inspiration, especially Joe Ciarrocchi, Gerry Fialkowski, Kelly Murray, Thomas Rodgerson, Kayliz Oakes, and Kevin Gillespie. They are my "manuscript readers" and the kind of cheerleaders everyone needs, especially during tough times.

Finally, I wish to express my deep appreciation to Joyce Rupp for taking time out from her demanding schedule to prepare a foreword. Given the focus of this work, I felt that the book would be "just right" if she were willing to provide a brief foreword to my discussion of prayerfulness. She agreed to this request and adds a tone only she can. Thanks, Joyce. It makes me happy to have your words in my little book.

# Introduction

Keeping God in the Conversation: Enhancing Prayerfulness in Your Spiritual Life

The key elements of spiritual intimacy in the time allotted to us on earth are fairly straightforward. They are, in order of importance:

Love God deeply,

Do what you can for others,

And, please, take good care of yourself.

But this, of course, is easier said than done. Such a life requires a heart filled with the cardinal virtue of humility and a growing desire for self-awareness. A full life also involves a willingness to serve others, rather than simply being wrapped up in ourselves, and—most important—a sense of spiritual mindfulness in our daily encounters so we can be open to the new lessons with which God continually graces us. Prayerfulness, in its purest form, is true receptivity to the essential lessons needed to live a full life. And, even when we are lost or resistant to a much-needed new perspective, spiritual mindfulness can actually position us to be surprised by grace. Let me illustrate.

1

In 2008, like so many others, I was caught in the middle of the dramatic downturn in the economy. I was concerned that I might not have enough cash on hand to provide support if someone in my family required it. Consequently, rather than selling only some of a small stock portfolio I had, I sold it all. It provided me with the cash on hand should my wife and I or a family member need some emergency funds. However, in the process of selling at a low point, I lost close to forty thousand dollars—a great deal of money to me! (It also didn't help my peace of mind that the next day the market jumped one thousand points.)

In response to my feelings of upset, my wife, Michaele, encouraged me to put it behind me with the thought that I had made the best decision I could given all of the factors I had to consider at the time. There were a number of truly more important things that were going on in my life at that point that really should have taken precedence. For instance, my two older brothers had recent brushes with serious illnesses. The brother closest to me in age wound up in the hospital for the first time in his life due to atrial fibrillation. Shortly after he was discharged, my oldest brother, who is already in a wheelchair, contracted an infection that affected his artificial heart valve, and he, too, was hospitalized for what would turn out to be a month-long stay. On top of all this, my daughter was also having a serious, renewed bout with asthma.

Yet, what continued to preoccupy me were not the illnesses of those close to me but the recent loss of money in the stock market. I knew in my head this was wrong. Very wrong. However, I could not seem to release myself from it no matter what psychological or spiritual approach I used. Finally, during one of my long walks I decided to put it in the hands of God.

I am a believer that the spiritual life is like a journey that passes through open fields and dense forests. When we are in the fields, we can travel across them with our own intuition, intelligence, and the help of our friends. We shouldn't expect God to do for us what we can do for ourselves. However, when we pass through the forests—the mystery of God—we are entering unfamiliar and often dark surroundings where only God can lead.

At this point I knew I was definitely in the forest, and I put my trust in God!

As I left my home and walked down the road, I waved to a neighbor. We passed the time for a bit, commenting on the weather because even though it was mid-October, it was a surprisingly warm and wonderful, sunny, Maryland fall afternoon. After walking a bit further, all the while admitting I could not seem to let go of my recent financial loss, a car pulled up next to me and the driver rolled down the window. It was the neighbor I had just chatted with minutes before.

She said, "There is something I want to share with you that I think you should know." Then she told me this story:

> Several years ago, a woman friend of mine was get-
> ting a divorce, and she asked if she could move in

with me for a few months. The few months became several years.

After leaving her husband she got involved with a man who I thought was a real loser. He was so bad that I would make sure I wasn't around when he visited. I also had a chance to meet her husband, who I thought was such a sweet guy.

At any rate, she came in the house one day and told me that she had run into you while you were doing some gardening in the yard and that you gave her one of your books. She later told me that after reading it, she felt that she was getting the message to go back with her husband. From what she took from the book she felt she and her husband needed to give it another chance, and that is just what she did!

After they were back together again for a few years, she discovered she had terminal-stage cancer. She died after a number of months, and her husband was at her side through it all. It was beautiful to see.

The reason I am sharing all of this with you is that you were a blessing to her when she needed it. A real blessing. Your spontaneous gift of one of your books was a surprising grace to her and her husband, and I just wanted to thank you from the bottom of my heart. *You* are indeed a blessing.

Well, when she started telling this story to me, I didn't know where she was going with it or why she was telling it to me. I barely knew her, and as the story proceeded, I only vaguely remembered giving her friend one of my books. But as she drove away, I could feel a new sense of perspective. I began to see more clearly what was really important in life. But, God was not through with me yet.

Later that night, I was amazed that a story shared by someone I barely knew, about an event I had long forgotten, had made such an impact on me. Yet, if I were being honest, a lot of precious energy was still being wasted on self-recrimination around my decision to sell some stock. When I was going to bed, I prayed, "What will it take to let me release this?" Then, as I lay there ready to fall asleep, I remembered something from over ten years ago.

A colleague in the pastoral counseling department in which I teach told me a story about a friend of his who was a very successful entrepreneur. As we sat together over lunch, he said to me, "As you know, my friend owns a number of prize horses and has even raced some of them in the Kentucky Derby. He was especially proud of one of his horses and anticipated making a fortune when he put him out to stud. Recently that horse broke its leg, and it had to be put to death."

"Wow, how is he doing with this loss of potentially millions of dollars?" I asked.

To which he replied, "Well, that's what I asked him, and in response he half smiled and said to me, 'I guess God was just keeping me in conversation as to what is really important in life.'"

As I recalled that story, the preoccupation about my own loss seemed to just melt. It was as if it were never important, certainly not as important as the health of my daughter, or my brothers, or the life story of my neighbor's friend. I was finally regaining a sense of spiritual perspective, and yet I knew it wasn't due to my own inner strength or wisdom. It was a grace given to me that I was grateful to receive and one that I certainly did not want to take for granted. (I had done that in the past a number of times and knew how disastrous that had been!)

The message was clear then and remains so now: even if we claim to be religious, a healthy spiritual perspective is neither automatic nor assured unless we are *spiritually mindful*. It is difficult to stay focused on what is truly important during the short life we have. The reality is that even if we are religiously committed, without even knowing it we can close our hearts to God's grace and the possibility of having a healthy perspective. Even worse, in some cases we may in our blindness believe that we are doing the right things and standing for the right principles in life.

A young priest and seminary faculty member once shared with me that he was worried about one of the men he was asked to mentor. In response, I asked if the man was taking out time in silence and solitude in chapel. I feel meditation is at the heart of the spiritual life, and when it is neglected, even the most generous, psychologically healthy person can become lost.

To my surprise he responded, "Yes. He religiously takes the time to pray, but when he leaves the chapel, he gossips about the faculty, is hurtful to many of his fellow students, and comes across in an arrogant way about what he believes is the only way to see certain things. Rather than attracting people to the Lord's loving presence, his sarcasm and certitude put people off."

After the mentor finished his story and as I was offering a few ideas on how this seminarian might be encouraged to look at some of his behaviors and attitudes, my mind went back to two other instances where the behavior of the persons didn't fit their religious commitment. One was a very religious older person who prayed the rosary regularly and went to daily Mass in her local Catholic church. However, despite her fervor, her family informed me that she was a very difficult person to be with. Any time someone would suggest that what she was doing was self-centered, she would respond harshly and say, "You just don't understand." As a result, she was persona non grata now in most of the healthcare facilities where she had been a patient over the past several years, and her sisters and one brother were estranged from her. Also, home-health aides hired to help her would quickly quit. Yet, despite all of this, she would constantly preach to whoever was present on the importance of having a close relationship with the Lord. The family was at its wit's end as to what to do since she had no insight into her style of interacting with others. There was little motivation for her to change since she was not under stress herself—but she certainly was a carrier!

Another example of this type of religious paradox was the case of a self-proclaimed Christian peace activist I had met. Being with him was anything but peaceful. Once, I remember sharing breakfast with him. He was so intense that every time he would say, "Pass the sugar!" it was like an incoming missile attack. As a matter of fact, when he finally got up to get himself another cup of coffee, the Irish priest who was eating with us looked up and said to me with a light brogue, "Glory be to God, Robert. Every time that boy speaks about peace, he scares the hell out of me!"

All of these people had never learned the truth of what St. Charles Borromeo said a long time ago: "Be sure that you first preach by the way you live. If you do not, people will notice that you say one thing but live otherwise." Although we might not have interpersonal styles that are as extreme or as noticeable as in the case of the young seminarian, the older devout Catholic woman, or the Christian peace activist described above, if we are honest, we will admit that all of us at times wear a set of spiritual blinders that can be hurtful to others. When this is so, it is often a lack of prayerfulness that prevents us from having our eyes fully open to the will of God in our daily interactions.

On the other hand, when we do seek to combine daily prayerfulness with meditation or contemplation, a "circle of grace" is formed that feeds, deepens, and enlivens our spiritual life. Then we can see clearly and act with love. Such a sense of spiritual awareness also helps us navigate the perils of spiritual intimacy that face anyone interested in having a rich interior life. It is only out of spiritual intimacy that we can live compassionately and meaningfully in today's anxious world. And so, while prayer must be at the heart of our spiritual life, if it is not simultaneously joined with prayerfulness, destructive spiritual and psychological pitfalls may remain unseen, uncorrected, and dangerous. In turn, our actions and attitudes may then become spiritually hurtful, rather than inspiring, for those we meet who need our help.

Still, avoiding such negativity by becoming more prayerfully aware in our daily activities is not so straightforward, even when we have a good mentor. When contemplative Thomas Merton was asked about offering others advice about their spiritual life, he responded, "No one can give you a map . . . your terrain is unique." Another wisdom figure also echoed this hesitation, but from a slightly different vantage point. He said, "If I tell you something, you will stick to it and limit your capacity to find out for yourself." However, to this a fellow spiritual guide countered, "[But] if the teacher says nothing, the students [will] wander about sticking to their habitual way of being." So, we need to avail ourselves of whatever and whomever we can in order to face ourselves and our lives in a loving, clear, spiritually mindful way.

So, exactly what are we to do to become more prayerful? I think Jesus gives us good direction on this in the Parable of the Sower (Mk 4:1–20), indicating the differences when the spiritual seed is able to land on good soil instead of rocky, thorny ground. The lesson clearly is that we must prepare our inner soil so we can be ready to receive the seeds that God so graciously sends us. The alternative can be to ignore and waste that gift of grace that is ever before us. As contemplative Thomas Merton wrote in *New Seeds of Contemplation*:

> Every moment and every event of every man's life on earth plants something in his soul. For just as the wind carries thousands of winged seeds, so each moment brings with it germs of spiritual vitality that come to rest imperceptibly in the minds and wills of men. Most of these unnumbered seeds perish and are lost, because men are not prepared to receive them; for such seeds as these cannot spring up anywhere except in the good soil of freedom, spontaneity and love.

How do we express our gratitude for the spiritual seeds we are given? How do we make the inner soil rich so we and those with whom we interact may benefit from them? In other words, what will aid in our "inner formation," what will equip us for the journey, no matter what terrain we might encounter at different phases of our life?

Inner Formation

Inner formation is not a set of techniques to be mastered. Rather, it is an ethos to be absorbed, an attitude to be cultivated. An abbot once alerted candidates about to enter a monastery, "There is no training here; it's just living the life so it gets 'into your bones, under your skin.'" Prayerfulness is the openness to let life get "into your bones, under your skin."

Inner formation is so important for us all because, really, when you come down to it, the quality of your life depends upon it. As physician and novelist Walker Percy once wrote, "What if life is like a train and I miss it?" When we lack prayerfulness, this becomes more possible than we might imagine.

Despite the reality of this, though, formation that spurs spiritual opportunity is often rejected because it requires *real attitudinal change*, a true alteration of the heart.

There is an ancient Indian fable that has been told in many forms over many years that relates this point well. My version is as follows:

> A mouse was constantly anxious because of its dread of a cat. An angel passing by saw this and pitied the poor creature. He then turned the mouse into a dog. Satisfied, he left, only to return several months later to find the dog now suffering from a paralyzing fear of a cheetah. Jumping in again, the angel changed the dog into a lion so it would be relieved once more of his anxiety. Upon returning months later, though, he found the lion now worried constantly about a rogue elephant that lived in the area. Finally, he turned the lion back into the mouse and said: "There is little anyone can do for you. Because no matter what changes are made outside, within you will always have the heart of a mouse."

The underlying attitude that will allow us to enhance our inner soil is offered to us in the simple words of Jesus: "Be like little children." Spiritual masters from the East sometimes refer to this as "beginner's mind." What might this mean in a practical sense for our purposes here? At the very least, several things come to mind with respect to children. First, there is a *transparency and honesty* that little children have that is not too common in most adults—even when it seems so. Secondly, there is a sensitivity to others that is touching and real, as we can see in the following story from a Catholic missionary:

> I was asked to give a talk to a group of first graders on what it was like to be a priest in Africa. One of them was my grandniece. After my talk to them, I sat with her on one side and her little friend on the other. We waited for the classes to be dismissed from the cafeteria where the talk was given. First the fourth grade was called up and formed two lines and left. Then the third grade. Then the second. Finally, just as they were about to call the first grade up to form two lines and leave, the little boy sitting on my left leaned over and whispered, "Do you want to get up and leave with us so you don't have to sit here all alone?"

Children also have a simplicity, hopefulness, and recognition of the importance of compassion that, at its core, is a central aspect of both caring for others and taking the next step in our own spiritual life. One child's reaction to a difficult situation reminds me of this. She was late coming home from school, and her mother was worried. When she finally stepped through the door, her mother yelled at her for being late, then caught herself, and asked, "Why were you late anyway?" To which the little girl responded, "I was helping a friend in trouble." "Well, what did you do to help her?" To which she replied quite simply, "I sat down next to her and helped her cry."

This child recognized a key element in the spiritual life that we as adults must not forget. If we do, the journey will lead to a dead end. She recognized that a faith-filled person must never turn her back on others but instead offer them a space to share their burdens. Such a healing space should not ever be underestimated. As novelist and minister Carl Frederick Buechner once noted, "They may forget what you said . . . but they will never forget how you made them feel." Or, in the words of spiritual guide David Brazier:

> [Our families, co-workers, and others] may come to us driven, depressed, stressed out, and angry, but [if we have the deep peace and joy of spiritual maturity] by not reacting, panicking, or jumping to conclusions, we break that cycle of negative drivenness by offering them a space to share their burden, and we help them recognize that this way of living need not be inevitable.

With this in mind, in the following chapters I will present guidance gleaned from classic and contemporary wisdom literature to enrich the inner soil. As a prelude to that guidance it is important to keep in mind three ways to approach this material (and other spiritual guidance you may receive) so the greatest possible change or inner formation can occur.

Three Approaches

First, to deepen our spiritual mindfulness, we must *attentively listen, read, and review the spiritual teachings* we wish to form us. They may come from sacred scripture, books, tapes, the lives of others, lectures, homilies, lessons, individual guidance, realizations received during meditation and quiet time alone, or the information in the following pages.

Second, we must be willing to "overlearn" what we have been taught so our ethos can be firmly formed by it. This takes time, effort, and study. Possibly, it means rereading our notes from a meeting we have had with a spiritual guide or considering a few lines we have written down about a homily we heard. Maybe it is a notation in our diary of an enlightening encounter or lines in a book that we highlighted for review later. Whatever it may be, we cannot assume we will remember or practice the lesson learned if it is not a part of our easily retrievable memory.

Third, the best way we can know for sure that the important spiritual teachings have taken root in us is to *practice, practice, practice*. With people we have just met, those we have as longtime friends, family, and those who seem to love or reject us, we must practice our lessons everyday. When we do this—not just in words but in actions—then we will experience what it is like to be on a real spiritual journey, not just one we idly dream about. One way to make this so is to realize that we are always surrounded by spiritual teachers *if only* we have the eyes to see them.

In a course on integrating psychology and spirituality, I once observed an unspoken reaction by one student toward another. The one student was outspoken, passionate, and even physically demonstrative when she was experiencing anger. The second student was quiet, somewhat reserved, and had a great deal of counseling experience.

When the passionate student would share a feeling or stridently make a point, the quiet student would make a face. The passionate student couldn't see it because she sat in the back of the room and he sat in the very front row. However, since I stood up front, I could easily notice it. After this happened again at the end of one class, I whispered to him as he was standing up to leave, "*She* is your spiritual director."

He looked at me somewhat surprised and said, "I'll certainly have to think about that."

"No," I replied calmly. "This is not something to think about. This is something to practice. She can be a powerful spiritual teacher for you if you let her be. She has much to teach you about yourself, and about how and why you react the way you do."

The Dalai Lama once said that he learned a great deal from those who differed from him in views or style, or even did not like him very much. They would tell him things others would not, and he benefited from their insights. So should we, when we encounter people like that in our lives.

The message then is: when we join a sense of prayerfulness with our intentional prayer in silence and solitude, our attitude will become transformed. Our whole life will then become our *spiritual* life. Without doing this, though, the perils of seeking spiritual intimacy with God in everyday life will often not be recognized. The results will not be good for us or for those in our family or circle of friends and acquaintances. When this happens, prayer will become narrow pietism and/or quietism. In instances such as this, our behavior and attitude will draw few to desire a closer relationship with God. Prayerfulness produces a sense of "spiritual mindfulness" even in the darkness of anxiety, doubt, loss, personal rejection, financial stress, anger, or sadness. With prayerfulness life can be an amazing learning experience not only for ourselves, but for those around us as well.

Completing the Circle of Grace

True spiritual awareness results from being in the present with your eyes wide open to experiencing life and God in dynamic new ways. This process may be formal (centering prayer, contemplation, meditation) or informal (an attentive attitude that keeps us awake to the moment and open to God). This attentiveness to how God and God's will are being revealed to us is what I have chosen to call "prayerfulness." Both the formal and informal aspects are important and interrelated. Contemplative Thomas Merton once pointed out that when we are mindful during the day, sitting down to meditate will not require a radical adjustment. Conversely, when we intentionally take out time in silence (and possibly solitude), we are more apt to have a greater sense of spiritual awareness during the rest of our day. And so, when prayer and prayerfulness are joined together in our lives, they form a positive circle of grace that can make a real difference in our lives.

Interestingly, even though this two-fold approach to being in the present with a real openness to experiencing life and God anew is both simple and powerful, it is not as welcomed as one would expect. Maybe this is so because it requires that we honestly face all of ourselves. This includes the negative thoughts, fears, doubts, desires, hypocrisies, and anxieties that often preconsciously lie just below our threshold of awareness. Seeing this information about ourselves may be initially disorienting or discouraging. We also may feel like Anne Lamott, who once said, "My mind is like a bad neighborhood. I don't want to go there alone." But go we must if we are to be free to experience *all* of our life and its epiphanies.

In the course of each day there are many opportunities to go deeper spiritually and to act more lovingly, just as there are many perils that can choke off our growth. If we are to find our way, we need to be spiritually mindful during the day as well as have special time apart, alone with God in meditation. Otherwise, we run the risk of merely listening to ourselves in our prayer and just thinking it is God.

This danger is not new. In the fourth century, many devoted persons went out to the desert to be with God and wound up simply spending time with their own egos. When this happened, some turned out to be harsh companions to their fellow monks. Some even went crazy. They certainly didn't become the dedicated spiritual *Ammas* (mothers) and *Abbas* (fathers) they were being called to be. The truth about ourselves that arises from deep prayer (and spiritual guidance) is sometimes very difficult to see and accept. Humility, while being the cardinal virtue of the desert, is very elusive—even if we have a role as a spiritual guide or religious leader. No one is exempt.

And so, in the following pages, there are words of support and challenge that require humility if they are to be absorbed. This virtue is essential so prayerfulness can lead to a form of freedom that allows us to see our gifts and growing edges with a sense of equanimity. As you read the following pages, make it your goal to embrace the spiritual themes that have been gleaned from both classic and contemporary wisdom. My hope is that you will view this material with a balance of clarity and kindness as you apply it to your life. The balance must be just right: too much clarity and you will hurt yourself (what psychodynamic psychologists call "narcissistic injury"). On the other hand, too much kindness and there will be little or no growth; instead, we will miss, gloss over, or too quickly excuse our behavior.

To help improve this delicate balance, each chapter ends with information for reflection on a specific aspect of prayerfulness. In addition, included in the second half of this book are a thirty-day personal retreat consisting of quotes, questions, and spiritual themes for reflection and prayer; and a brief Spiritual Mindfulness Questionnaire (SMQ) with a commentary to help in the consideration of your responses. The goal of these "navigation guides" is to help you bring to life the spiritual gifts you have been given in your daily activity. This will in turn help to enrich your time alone with God and lead to a more compassionate life. Without such personalization, reflection, and the action it can lead to, the information in this book will remain only at the level of thought and change little, if anything, in the way you live.

There is always so much more for us in our spiritual lives. You have probably taken a lot of good steps already. Yet, there is so much more to know and live that it would be a shame not to avail yourself of what can help you to experience each day more prayerfully. William Paulsell, in his book *Rules for Prayer*, writes:

> It may be that you consider prayer as being more than simply just asking God for things you want.... You may have developed certain disciplines, setting aside time for prayer on a regular basis. You now pray frequently, having integrated prayer into your normal routine. . . . You offer prayer of praise, thanksgiving, confession and intercession. You have also

begun to meditate on scripture and to ponder more carefully things you have often taken for granted or practiced by rote.

But still something is lacking. . . . [You're] doing all the right things and making a sincere effort, often at the sacrifice of the elements that once were important in your life. However, God still seems very distant, and while you feel good about yourself for living a more disciplined religious life, you still wonder if there is something more that ought to be happening.

A serious spiritual life is more than just following the rules and doing things the proper way. More fundamental is the attitude with which we enter into and carry on our quest.

This attitude is formed by the dramatic commitment to joining prayerfulness with periods of formal prayer each day. This will not only help you avoid the personal perils you encounter, but also open you up so much more to the freedom, peace, and joy of the interior life. So, it is with this hope in mind that we turn next to look at and reflect upon some of these very essential guides to enriching our sense of "the spiritual" each day. To set the stage, take a moment or two of silent prayerful reflection after reading the following, well-loved prayer by Thomas Merton (from his *Thoughts in Solitude*):

I have no idea where I am going. I do not see the road ahead of me. I cannot know for certain where it will end. Nor do I really know myself, and the fact that I think that I am following your will does not mean that I am actually doing so. But I believe that the desire to please you does in fact please you. And I hope that I will never do anything apart from that desire. And I know that if I do this, you will lead me by the right road, though I may know nothing about it. Therefore will I trust you always, though I may seem to be lost and in the shadow of death. I will not fear, for you are ever with me, and you will never leave me to face my perils alone.

ONE

Navigating the Perils of Spiritual Intimacy

To tack a boat, to sail a zigzag course, is not to deny our destination or our destiny—despite how it may appear to those who never dare to take the tiller in their hand. Just the opposite: It's to recognize the obstacles that stand between ourselves and where we want to go, and then to maneuver with patience and fortitude, making the most of each leg of our journey, until we reach landfall.

—**Richard Bode**
First You Have to Row a Little Boat

Create Simple Rituals

Rituals help us to be spiritually mindful of what is before us by focusing our attention on the task at hand. Thus, rituals can transform simple acts into sacred experiences. When as a young man I lived for a year in the Ryukyu Islands off the coast of Japan, I had a chance to see this for myself during an educational trip to Tokyo and Kyoto.

While there I attended a tea ceremony where I was the only non-Asian in the room. As I learned the steps involved in following the ritual, the beauty and sacredness of preparing and serving tea came to life. This sense has never left me.

Such rituals can be healing when true spiritual mindfulness is present and we feel gratitude to the Lord for offering us life in such wonderful refreshing ways. This is important to realize because rituals not only make the ordinary sacred, they also can support us during difficult times.

The rituals need not be elaborate, just done regularly, performed with the right spirit, and—as in the case of all Christian forms of prayerfulness—intentionally done in the presence of God.

One such ritual for me starts very early each morning. At about 4:30 or 5:00 a.m., I get up and make coffee, pour myself a cup, and return to bed to sit there quietly on my propped up pillows for half an hour. This simple relaxed time with the Lord is the perfect way for me to start the day. In good times and bad, this remains for me an opportunity to center myself and turn my day over to God.

Following this, I get another cup for myself and one for my wife Michaele, who is rising about this time to start her day. We then take at least a half hour to chat and begin the day. We share our thoughts and ideas as well as read the day's scriptural passages before I go off to shower and she crosses the hall for her period of prayer. Both the time alone with God and time together with God at our side has always made a big difference and still does today in our marriage. It is how we greet each day.

Another simple ritual is taking a short walk alone each day. This time provides a chance to experience life and helps to nurture prayerfulness. Walking mindfully with God has a long tradition in Christianity, formal and informal. Without such rituals, life can easily get out of hand and become an experience of rushing toward our grave until an event that reminds us of what's important steps in and stops us in our tracks, asking: "Where are you going? Life is so short. Are you being mindful, loving, and attentive to yourself and those around you? Are you attending in various ways to the peace of God within you?"

In his book *The Genesee Diary*, spiritual writer Henri Nouwen asks two core questions that all of us will confront again and again in life's journey:

> Is there a quiet stream underneath the fluctuating affirmations and rejections of my little world? Is there a still point where my life is anchored and from which I can reach out with hope and courage and confidence?

When I visited Henri a long time ago in his little apartment off Harvard Square, I asked him if there was one thing I should do to center myself as I greeted each day—especially given the challenging work I was facing. At the time, as is now the case, I was dealing with a special kind of darkness that is being experienced by helping and healing professionals such as psychologists, persons in full-time ministry, social workers, physicians, nurses, relief workers, statespersons, teachers, and others.

He hesitated before responding and then simply advised me to follow this simple ritual: take out time each morning to read scripture—maybe the reading of the day—and then with that nestled in my heart, remain quiet for twenty minutes. It's almost twenty-five years since he gave me that advice, and I have remained faithful to it in some form since that time.

Being wrapped in silence, solitude, and gratitude with powerful words of scripture can center and guide us through the day in a way that offers us "an anchor," "still point," or "nest" to both return to and from which to reach out. Moreover, when we take such a daily journey, it can also educate us to look at life with a sense of prayerfulness. This then can set the stage for awe to take precedence over simply manipulating our existence as best we can in an effort to gain more pleasure and comfort. Simple rituals of prayerfulness balance the secular obsession with success, fame, power, physical attractiveness, money, or simply getting our way. They help prevent such normal human desires from becoming idols.

This is a lesson that we need to learn for ourselves, and one that we also need to pass on to our children. In the words of Rabbi Abraham Joshua Heschel:

> We teach children how to measure, how to weigh. We fail to teach them how to revere, how to sense wonder and awe. The sense of the sublime, the sign of the inward greatness of the human soul and something which is potentially given to all . . . is now a rare gift.

Maybe the source of wonder is something obvious that wakes us up. For instance, when St. Louis Parish in Clarksville, Maryland, was building a new church, they had reached the point where they were elevating the corpus of Christ up onto the cross behind the altar. As they slowly lifted it, spontaneously the construction workers present stopped what they were doing, became silent, and took off their hats as a sign of respect. It was an unexpected moment of awe for those who had the eyes to see it that way.

Such spiritually mindful moments are epiphanies if we let them be. They may even introduce us in a very profound way to the meaning and symbolism that we have missed at a deep level all along.

One such moment occurred at the Daylesford Norbertine Abbey in Paoli, Pennsylvania, when a priest from their religious order visiting from India led the liturgy. At Mass, just prior to the consecration when he would utter the words of Christ, "This is my Body. This is my Blood," he would take off his shoes. This simple ritual of deep respect by someone from a different culture opened the eyes of the people in attendance to what was about to happen. It renewed what may have been a long lost sense of wonder.

Signs of awe may also be quite simple in our daily experience. We often get "messages from heaven" and miss them because we fail to respect and be awake to them. What are some of these "messages"?

A child's laugh,
Snow falling on snow,
A light grip of our arm by a smiling elder,
The sound of rain on the roof,
The crash of waves,
The rustling of trees in the wind.

But once again we must we aware of what is happening. Our eyes must be open to experience them. In the story of the Transfiguration of Jesus, the apostles experienced something wonderful "because they had stayed awake" (Lk 9:32). We must be present, mindful, open, and awake in the same way. Simple rituals can keep us from going to sleep during such daily epiphanies.

Once when in Florida, I visited Captiva, where the sunsets are said to be among the most beautiful in the world. With just a few entertaining cumulus clouds forming fascinating shapes, the dark blue sky was the perfect backdrop to the sunset we had experienced. Then just after it set, a young man came running down to the edge of the beach complaining to all of his friends and noting all the reasons he was late. It really didn't matter what he had to say, the bottom line was, he wasn't there. He had the chance. He chose poorly. He missed it.

Spirituality, if it is to be real, must encourage awareness of these experiences. Simple rituals can create a *discipline of holy attention*. As Henri Nouwen noted in one of his classic works, *Making All Things New*:

> The beginning of the spiritual life is often difficult not only because the powers which cause us to worry are so strong but also because the presence of God's Spirit seems barely noticeable. If, however, we are faithful to our discipline, a new hunger will make itself known.

Indian Jesuit priest, psychologist, and Eastern writer Anthony de Mello echoed this theme in the lively way for which he was known. In the following dialogue from his collection of spiritual sayings from around the world, he reminds us that while we must remember that God's grace, not our will, produces spiritual insight, it still doesn't relieve us of the need to be spiritually mindful. We must exhibit a grateful readiness to receive these gifts:

> The disciple asks, "Is there anything I can do to make myself enlightened?"
>
> To which the spiritual master responds, "As little as you can do to make the sun rise in the morning."
>
> "Then of what use are the spiritual exercises you prescribe?"
>
> "To make sure you are not asleep when the sun begins to rise."

Simple rituals can ensure that we are spiritually awake. They also set the stage for important learning during the difficult times in our life, "if only we have the eyes to see." On the other hand, "mindlessness" not only keeps us blind to all that we should be grateful for, but also prevents us from being all that we can truly be—no matter what is going on in our life at any given time. And so, as part of our journey to become more spiritually awake, we must be able to pick up and attend to "the red flags of mindlessness."

Spiritual Suggestion: *Become more aware of spiritual mindlessness.*

To love God with your whole heart and mind—in the words of Irenaeus, a Father of the Church—is to be a "human person fully alive." But to be fully alive we must be spiritually aware and living in the present moment with our eyes and heart wide open to God's presence, even in unexpected and possibly unfamiliar ways.

When we are prayerful, we take the time to quiet ourselves in little ways so we can attend to God's presence during our daily interactions and thus avoid the natural tendency to be "spiritually mindless" at times. When we live without a sense of God's presence in our lives, we miss a lot and waste a good deal of energy. However, we can more quickly and prayerfully return to "the now" when we are able to recognize those red flags that indicate when we are not spiritually aware of what God is offering and teaching us. It is helpful to acknowledge our mindlessness when:

- we get easily upset—often over the wrong things—and miss what life is offering us in all interactions and events;
- interruptions are seen only as disruptive rather than informative or possible, unexpected opportunities;
- habits and rules continue to sap life's freshness for us;
- we spend too much time in the silver casket of nostalgia or rushing through precious moments of our lives under the impression that living this way is "only practical";
- we only fantasize about "the spirit of simplicity" and "letting go" rather than seeking to practice them more in our lives;
- our promises to ourselves to adopt a healthier lifestyle don't translate into the necessary actions;

- we spend so much of the time in a cognitive cocoon of judgment, worry, preoccupation, resentment; fear, and regret that we miss life's daily gifts happening all around us;
- our time in silence and solitude often ends up being boring and emotionally flat rather than renewing;
- we seem to ignore the spiritual gifts of laughter, a child's smile, or a good conversation and instead focus on increasing such trivial things as fame, power, security, and pleasure;
- a cancelled get-together, a brief illness, or a delay in our schedule is not appreciated as a spontaneous period for spiritual mindfulness;
- transitions make up much of our life but are not seen as being as valuable as our destinations;
- the "ghosts" of our past memories are not valued as the teachers they can be, but instead merely serve to pull us down or fill us with regret;
- a sense of intrigue or curiosity about ourselves— including both our gifts and growing edges—is overshadowed by our self-blame, discouragement, or projecting faults onto others;
- too much of our lives is spent running away from what we don't like or in "medicating" ourselves, seeking security, or grasping, rather than simply enjoying and being grateful for all that is around us;
- sincerity, transparency, and being a person without guile seems absent even though we know we waste

so much unnecessary energy on being defensive, wearing interpersonal masks, or seeking to manipulate others;

- we rush around like a gargoyle on roller skates while failing to notice people we have hurt, what we are eating, how we are feeling, or even what we are really doing or supposed to be paying attention to (such as the road when we are driving a car or the person to whom we are supposed to be paying attention).

When we behave in such mindless ways, we can simply return to being spiritually mindful by following this simple ritual: take a breath, lean back into the present, and look to see where God might be present in what we are encountering. Surprisingly, such awareness may not result in the alleviation of pain or the uncomfortable feelings we are experiencing at the time or even in the receipt of the specific gift which we are requesting or expecting. But, it may result in a new perspective and freedom we previously didn't have, yet need, for the next phase of our life; and this may be even more important than instant relief.

Henri Nouwen recognized this when he wrote in *Making All things New*,

"What is new is that we no longer experience the many things, people, and events as endless causes for worry, but begin to experience them as the rich variety of the ways in which God makes his presence known to us. When our hearts are set on that kingdom, our worries will slowly move to the background, because the many things which made us worry so much start to fall into place.

We begin to truly understand the question, "What does it mean to set our hearts on the kingdom?" We begin to see that prayerfulness helps us become more spiritually aware so we can shift our lives into "psychological reverse." And so, when we become preoccupied with the future, get caught up in our failures, and our minds become filled with our own needs, greeds, and obsessions, we can, with a sense of prayerfulness, lean back and join God in the present. As we pay attention to what is going on around and in us, we will truly begin to know that all, indeed, will be well.

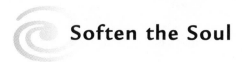# Soften the Soul

Prayerfulness does not always remove the pain in our lives but may open up new vistas that lead to a "softening of our soul." When this occurs, amazing things can happen in our own lives as well as those of our families, friends, and even casual acquaintances.

Shortly after I received my doctorate, there was a man of about forty whom I had the privilege of mentoring. He would often come in and explore with me different turns in his life that he felt would bring him closer to God. He rarely complained, and what pain he did seem to encounter he was able to integrate in his life through a prayerful spirit.

On one of his visits he seemed different. It was the expression on his face and his way of being. I couldn't put my finger on it but there was something there. I didn't know exactly what I was picking up, so I said, "Today, you seem different in some way." He responded with a half smile and after a moment said, "I feel both sad and clear. Maybe that is what you are picking up." He then went on to tell me this story:

> A few days ago I overheard my wife speaking with
> her closest friend about our neighbor, who had

discovered that her husband was having an affair. My wife said how upset the woman was and how, upon discovering this, a light went out in her life.

We had a similar problem shortly after we got married and before our three children were born. She discovered that I was having an affair with a friend at work. That was almost twenty years ago. Since then I think we have moved on and have an even better marriage. However, when I heard her say that about our neighbor, it made me realize that when my wife found out about my affair, a light had gone out in her life as well.

After hearing his story, I asked, "What was your reaction when you realized that?"

He responded, "I felt deeply sad, too. I guess a light went out in my life as well at that point. You see, I had thought it was all forgotten, but nothing is ever totally forgotten; nor should it be, I guess. Otherwise, we'd never learn or see our mistakes and sins clearly enough to appreciate the value of humility. However, amidst this sense of sorrow and regret, I also remembered what we had been working on here in our sessions. I thought this was a good time to also include this sadness in my mindfulness prayer."

"What happened?"

"Well, rather than running away from this unpleasant reality like I had done with so many things in the past by rationalizing what I had done, workaholism, alcohol abuse, or even a form of what I thought was prayer to cover it all up or excuse myself, I just sat with the Lord and quietly looked straight at what I had done and the terrible results of it."

"Any change?"

"I think so. I'd like to think it made me realize that in this action I had caused pain in a person I loved. Somehow, as I sat with the negative reality of this in my life, I didn't run away this time. Yet, because of what I had learned about mindfulness prayer from our sessions, I didn't just beat myself up either. I simply faced my life directly, and I think God softened my soul in the process. Of course, I am still thoughtless at times in other smaller ways with people I care for, but I think I am able to pick up my failures more quickly now and do something about them. It may sound crazy, but in a good way I keep this past infidelity before my eyes."

As he shared his sad story, an experience of the Dalai Lama came to mind. He had been planning to ordain a number of monks to a new rite. One of them was an older monk, and the Dalai Lama decided against including him because he felt that the rigorous process would be too exhausting for his frail body. Shortly before the ceremony he was told by an aide that the monk responded by committing suicide. His hope was that he would be reincarnated and then as a young man would be able to take on this ordination in his next life.

When an interviewer who learned of this event years later asked the Dalai Lama how he got over such a sad event, the Dalai Lama looked at him and with a puzzled expression said as he tapped the spot over his heart, "Get over it? Why, it is still with me."

The question is, though, *how* was it with him? When we are sad about something someone has done to us or something we have done, thought, or felt, *how* we embrace these shameful, unfortunate mistakes or realities that may have caused direct or unforeseen harm to others makes all the difference. Being prayerful and awake to God's presence in our lives certainly doesn't take away the pain or the guilt—nor should it—but it does something with our negative experiences so we can learn, deepen, grow, and maybe even soften.

We can experience guilt in two basic ways. The first is what I term "impure guilt." It has us recognize our failings or sins and then pulls us into the past and leaves us there. We are then caught and psychologically buried in a way that may induce us to ignore, excuse, or defensively run away from having to face our negative realities. "Pure guilt," on the other hand, occurs when we face our errors clearly and directly but without a crippling sense of judgment. Instead we have the love of God by our side so we can repent and learn from the errors. Then, with newfound humility, we can seek greater holiness in the present and future. This process also helps us to deepen our commitment as people and spiritually softens us so we can be more compassionate to others—and *ourselves*. And so, given this, it is important that we know as much as we can about being prayerful—being in the present with our eyes wide open to experiencing God and life in dynamic new ways. In this way, our lives can be more joyous, ethical, compassionate, and meaningful.

After reflecting on the Dalai Lama's experience and the young man's story of a light going out in his wife's life, I recalled the following couple of lines from the Coelho novel *The Alchemist*: "The dunes are changed by the wind, but the desert never changes. That's the way it will be with our love for each other." When we are prayerful, love for God, love for those we have hurt, and even love for those who may have hurt us can be the last word. That is the promise of the prayerful life.

We all make mistakes—sometimes big ones—but there is always an opportunity for love to grow from these regrettable acts when we are open to letting the Lord teach us. But there are two questions we must answer: Will we clearly recognize our faults and through God's love let a freeing, renewing grace come to us? Can we have patience and be as compassionate with ourselves as we are or need to become with others?

Prayerful patience brings doubt and hope together. When we allow ourselves to experience this during the uncertain periods of our life—those that are neither black and white nor in living color but are gray—we are free to move in new directions. This reality is especially brought forth in the following personal story shared by a young woman in training to become a pastoral counselor:

> From my own life experience, I can attest to the fact that it is truly hard to believe something positive can

come out of the deep despair we are going through in the moment we are in that place of darkness. Having struggled myself with periods of anxiety and depression at different points in my life, I am all too familiar with the spiritual darkness that has sought to be my companion on the journey. How many times have I sat in church on a dark day wishing the pastor would save the sermon for someone who cares?

I was running from God's word, myself, and others; fighting so hard to keep my head above water, yet feeling constantly pulled under by the currents of life. I wanted to be strong, secure, and self-assured. Where is that spiritual water that once quenched my inner thirst? Where is the God who pursued me to the point of salvation? Yet, as one author notes, it is in "recognizing our fragility, helplessness, alienation, deep sadness, and being lost that surprisingly we will experience a sense of peace." This statement rang true for me when I went back to the therapist I was seeing *after* I had completed the ten hours of required growth therapy that was part of my education in pastoral counseling. I was fighting so hard not to feel my emotions, denying the reality of my ambivalence toward my current circumstances, filled with pride about returning to her, and filled with self-hatred for being so "weak" in having to go back for counseling.

However, the ten hours of "required" therapy had only begun to stir the pot. Now the stove had been turned up and the pot was on full boil.

In one particular session in therapy I was feeling distraught and said to the therapist helplessly, "When am I finally going to be my most authentic self?" She paused and then softly said back to me, "Maybe this is your authentic self. Maybe it's who you are right now." That comment stuck with me. I thought to myself, "You mean right *now* with all the pain, turmoil, and ambivalence that I feel everyday?" I realized that my most authentic self was not the strong Christian woman who always knew her purpose and calling, who walked in total obedience to God. I saw I was deceived about what it meant to be authentic. Suddenly I felt like I was in a "spiritual delivery room" filled with anticipation for the arrival of a new baby—the gift God had given me now to walk in authenticity and self-acceptance.

Even though it is at the heart of prayerfulness, patience is undervalued today. But this was not always so. St. Francis de Sales used to advise persons who sought his guidance that people need "a cup of understanding, a barrel of love, and an ocean of patience." Would that we could have such a sense of prayerfulness filled with such patient compassion with ourselves. Our lives, and the lives of those who count on us, would be so much better for it. And so, as we embrace a new sense of what prayerfulness can be for us, it would be helpful for us to always remember that welcoming the gift of patience should be in our hearts as well.

Spiritual Suggestion: *Seek to be patient and compassionate with every event and person you encounter—including yourself!*

From John's gospel, we hear Jesus promise that he will bring us "fullness" (Jn 10:10), "not leave us orphaned but come back for us" (Jn 14:18), and that he now calls us "friend" (Jn 15:15). With these deeply encouraging and hopeful images in mind, take out a few moments in silence and solitude.

- Welcome your feelings of regret, loneliness, sadness, loss, and secret shame. Greet your fears and anxieties with the same kindness with which God greets you each morning as you wake and meet the day.
- Welcome your failings, sinful habits, whatever you may be trying to hide (even from God!). Welcome too your seeming inability to let go of self-condemnation, to forgive others, to trust in spiritual intimacy, and to greet each day with receptivity and openness to the movement of God in your life.

As you do this again and again, picture God holding out a hand to you to bring you along into the next place in your life—"the now"—so you can resume your life in a different and lighter way that demonstrates a deeper friendship with yourself.

When we are truly prayerful, we change our relationship with the dark places in our lives. Instead of giving up, hiding from, fixing, or rejecting them, we face them with the Lord by our side and learn from them in a way that allows our souls to soften, our compassion to become deeper, and our appreciation of God's forgiving and loving heart to become greater. What more can we ask than that? And, in the end, isn't that much better for us and those in our lives than the negative alternatives?

Honor Life's Fragility

When we are continuously aware of life's fragility, we are more spiritually mindful and life is richer. Psychiatrist Mark Epstein tells a story about a visit he and other mental health professionals made to the revered wisdom figure Ajahn Chah in Thailand. They were in discussion with him about spiritual mindfulness, impermanence, and gratitude for life, when at one point Ajahn Chah looked at them and held up a glass. He said, "You see this glass. I love this glass. It holds water. It is beautiful when the sun shines through it. It makes a nice ping sound when you hit it. But if the wind blows through the window and knocks it over and it breaks . . . *of course!* When I know the glass is already broken, I love every minute I have it." Obviously, he is raising our minds to the fact that fragility is true not only with respect to our possessions, but also of our relationships. For the life we have on this earth is precious and short. Prayerfulness leads us to remember this and honor life's fragility, to value what and who is really important in our lives in a more sensitive way.

When my daughter was thirty-five years old, she called and told me she hadn't been feeling well for quite a while. I asked whether she was going to visit the doctor. In response, she told me she already had and was referred to a pulmonologist. Later that week she telephoned with the report from him: "He said I have diminished blood flow in the left ventricle, pulmonary hypertension, a mass in my lung, and evidence of pulmonary emboli."

After asking how she felt after hearing all of this and what the planned medical treatment was, I took a step back so I wouldn't be upset in the moment. That would be useless to her. I then reframed the experience for her so she could keep her anxiety in check. I told her I would feel the same sense of shock if it had happened to me but was glad she finally had a physician that had given her a full diagnosis and treatment plan. I then let her express her feelings some more and told her that her mom and I would call again later that night.

When I got off the phone, I sat there for a while and realized (yet once again!) how fragile life is. I recognized that repeatedly in life, when we don't keep this in mind, we discover how easy it is to lose perspective. We rush mindlessly toward our graves. Filled with myriad desires and activities, we usually walk around in an envelope of thought. We are in the future, preoccupied with details, or captured in the past. In the process we miss the people and experiences around us until it is too late for us or for them. Even when we go for a quiet walk, we are often really going out for "a think." We are so filled with resentments, desires, plans, shames, worries, and feelings of anxiety that we fail to experience the walk. We come home without having seen, smelled, or listened to anything or anyone who crossed our paths. Jon Kabat-Zinn in his modern classic work, *Wherever You Go, There You Are*, puts forth this situation well when he notes:

> If what happens now does influence what happens next, then doesn't it make sense to look around a bit from time to time so that you are more in touch with what is happening now, so that you can take your inner and outer bearings and perceive with clarity the path that you are actually on and the direction in which you are going? If you do so, maybe you will be in a better position to chart a course for yourself that is truer to your inner being—a soul path, a path with heart, *your* path with a capital P. If not, the sheer momentum of your unconsciousness in this moment just colors the next moment. The days, months, and years quickly go by unnoticed, unused, unappreciated. . . .
>
> No one else can do this job of waking up for us, although our families and friends do sometimes try desperately to get through to us, to help us see more clearly or break out of our own blindness. But waking up is ultimately something that each one of us can only do for ourselves. When it comes down to it, wherever *you* go, there *you* are. It's *your* life that is unfolding.

This experience of my grown daughter's health problems brought me back to when my daughter was nine years old and she required an operation for scoliosis. She had bone chipped off her hips, thirteen levels of her spine fused, and a stainless steel rod inserted to stabilize her spine. It woke me up to what I felt was really important at the time, and I thought this wake-up call would last for the rest of my life. However, as I could see now from this recent call from her, my insight back then into life's fragility clearly did not remain as a beacon for now.

And so, I think an important lesson is that true prayerfulness is not captured once and for all but must be continually embraced. A few quiet moments spent in the morning, afternoon, and evening reflecting on the fragility of the people and other gifts life offers us would seem to be a sensible and gentle first step toward changing our relationship with all aspects of life. The following story told to me by a young woman in her twenties who experienced a tragedy that led to awakening shows that prayerfulness can even positively alter our spiritual maturity level. The result: we welcome a spiritual adulthood out of which we can live rather than remaining childish in our faith.

In her case, she was taught as a parochial grade school student that you encounter God through prayer. For her this meant the sign of the cross at the beginning of prayer was like dialing the telephone; the sign of the cross at the end of prayer was like hanging up the receiver. Like many of her peers, she was in graduate school before she even took the time to reflect about this; she thought she still believed it.

After reflection, she realized that while the telephone metaphor was age-appropriate when she first learned it, something deeper should be possible with time. However, while she supposed on a certain level she knew her spirituality had changed from elementary school, she didn't see how far it had come or how much further it could go. A reason for this is that she rarely set out to change her spirituality from what it was in childhood. Yet, perhaps her previous, fragile, juvenile sense of God had to break before a stronger, more mature and authentic one could have a place to grow. It is as if (in her words) "the seeds of spirituality needed to look for the freshly tilled soil of broken-open souls."

For her first twenty years, spirituality had little import in her life beyond being part of her tradition. Adopting the values of Catholicism because her parents told her that they were good and attendance at Sunday Mass were the extent of her religious activities and faith. She lived in peaceful and happy surroundings, life caused more joy than pain, more laughs than tears, more good than bad. She saw a limited need for encounters with God. She saw a limited need for daily prayer. At this time in her life, she supposed that her spirituality could afford to stay in a cerebral space where God existed on Sunday mornings and on occasion in evening prayer. Then something happened that shifted everything. What she had constructed as her solid ground became a seismic spiritual wave underneath her previously rooted feet. It happened suddenly when she received a phone call that her youngest brother, seventeen years old at the time, had suddenly disappeared.

In her own words:

> Thomas, my brother, was participating in a group glacier expedition in Alaska. I was told that he had broken off into a small group with two other young men. They had completed a strenuous eight-hour hike—one of many over the previous twenty-nine days that they had been on the glacier. The group he was in was tired, thirsty, and in need of setting up camp and cooking dinner on what was to be their last night on the glacier before group members were to say good-bye and return to their respective homes.
>
> Thomas offered to collect water while the other two young men set up tents. Prior to doing this, he removed his hiking pack, picked up two tin buckets, and walked off, in search of water . . . never to be seen again.
>
> One bucket was recovered near a drainage hole in a glacier, known as a crevasse. Looking back, it is believed that while attempting to fill one bucket from a small stream of water near the top of the crevasse, Thomas slipped, falling thousands of feet into the interior of the glacier. Many attempts were made to recover his body; all proved unsuccessful. Faced with a reality too far removed from what I had previously constructed as real, into the depths of the crevasse, too, fell my understanding of life.

I remember traveling to Alaska, each family member coming from different parts of the U.S. at different times within a twenty-four-hour period. I left when there was still hope that Thomas would be found. My eldest brother left at a time when hope was slipping away. My mother, my father, another brother, and sister boarded a plane to Alaska when prayers of remaining hope turned to prayers for the recovery of the remains of the dead.

It was upon word of this reality, in a field outside the base camp of the glacier expedition, that I literally fell to my knees. I placed my head in my hands. For the first time in my life, I felt completely empty. I see now how for the first time in my life, I felt like I had an honest prayer to pray: "God, please greet Thomas in heaven."

I remember, too, traveling home from Alaska. My sister and I had been given the task of carrying Thomas's hiking pack back home. The pack was heavy. It took the strength of both my sister and me together to move the pack across the Anchorage airport. Perhaps because of the shape of the bag, the color, the weight, or for the reason that the bag possessed all that was materially left of Thomas, I felt as if I was carrying my brother's body. I carried this image in my heart, returning home.

Her brother Thomas's body was never recovered. She reported that her spirituality risked the same disappearance.

She questioned everything around his death, from the possibility of his still being alive to the possibility of him never really having existed. She asked the same spectrum of questions of the reality of God: "Is God still alive? Did God ever exist?" Spiritually, she was broken. She was encountering God at this time "in a very raw way." She had no more time for politely dialing some metaphorical prayer phone like she did as a child.

Surprisingly, and wonderfully, all of these spiritual cul-de-sacs led her to encounter God each second of the day instead of abandoning her relationship with God. She said, "We had conversations nearly every instance of the day." She recognized that she was beginning to truly own her spiritual identity and was taking God out of the box where she had him. She could now encounter him *everywhere*. She did this because, in her own words, "If I didn't, how else could I comprehend the incomprehensible act of my brother's death other than enveloped in the embrace of God?"

Encountering God in this way led to some subsequent surprising encounters with God's healing presence. These led to new experiences of perspective and even joy. One of the ways was that after her brother Thomas died, it was as if the people of the town she lived in opened their lives to her in previously unimaginable ways. Many people began telling her their own stories of love and loss in ways that she felt not only a sense of solidarity with them, but also greater impetus to lead a more actively compassionate life.

A remarkable tragedy, and an openness amidst her sadness, did not eliminate or play down her sorrow or loss. Nothing could do that. But it did lead her to greater meaning in her life and a sense of God that might never have otherwise been found. Yet, as we will see in the next chapter, for all of this to happen we must be willing to face *all* of our life—including, maybe especially, our dark times—*directly*. And to do this, there is no greater approach than prayerfulness. So, it would benefit us at this point to take a few moments before moving on, to reflect deeply on some of the characteristics of living a prayerful life. It is a very helpful way of being aware of what spiritual and psychological wonders await us when we consciously walk through our day with the Lord at our side.

Spiritual Suggestion: *Reflect on the essential characteristics of prayerfulness.*

There are unique characteristics of prayerfulness that can help you mature spiritually. Knowing them encourages you to "break open" the dramatic and daily occurrences of your life in order to welcome the Spirit of God's activity in deeper, more creatively nourishing ways at each stage. Putting these characteristics into practice will help you keep in mind life's fragility and appreciate each day. Some of the characteristics of prayerfulness especially worth remembering include:

- a clear awareness of what you are experiencing, thinking, or feeling without judging yourself or others;

- a sense of intrigue about yourself and others without projection (blaming others), self-condemnation, discouragement, or expectations;
- more interest in discovering the presence of grace—namely the wonderful gifts of God—rather than merely focusing on your accomplishments;
- an appreciation of being in the now and a willingness to return to the present when you are drawn into the past or begin to be preoccupied by the future;
- a spirit of "unlearning" and a willingness to see life differently that is inspired by the lord's call to "make all things new;"
- a non ego-centered approach to life that recognizes it isn't all about *me*;
- a willingness to recognize, embrace, and flow with change;
- a spirit of receiving life as it is without reaction or rejection;
- gratitude and an openness to being nourished by God in everyday life;
- a focus on those activities that create well-being instead of suffering for others . . . and *ourselves*;
- appreciation of the beauty of patience and enjoying the process of life rather than solely looking forward to completions or successes;
- an interest in letting go of the "secular training" we have received in grasping, being envious, angry, and unkind, and instead an openness to sharing without

an expectation of getting anything in return, being intrigued by our responses so we can learn from them rather than responding by being defensive or self-indicting, and slowing down rather than straining toward goals (even perceived good ones);

- avoidance of comparing ourselves favorably or unfavorably with others;
- a greater desire to be sensitive to how our words and actions affect others;
- openness to "spiritually touching" all of our denials, loneliness, shame, and negative feelings about ourselves with compassion, rather than running away from them;
- allowing information, negative and positive, familiar and unfamiliar, to flow to us without being obstructed or modified by our ego or fears;
- an increased desire for transparency and being persons without guile in the way we live so we can help purify—rather than contaminate with our defensiveness—the spiritual atmosphere in which we and others live.

Practicing, not just knowing about, these characteristics of prayerfulness results in your getting all out of the life that God gives you as a gift. In addition, and of possibly even more importance, doing this will help you face life's difficulties, gray periods, or sad experiences and deepen you in ways you may never have dreamed possible. This will be a gift to those with whom you come into contact as well.

Face Sadness Directly

At different turning points in their lives, people may undergo the significant experience that John of the Cross termed "the dark night of the soul." Others of us may undergo periods of clinical depression that require psychological treatment and possibly medication. But *all of us*, no matter who we are and what our roles are in life, experience times of fleeting or prolonged sadness. Becoming more fully aware of our sadness, as well as what this experience might prayerfully hold for us, can actually determine the quality of our overall life. And so, *how and with whom* we approach such common, often poignant, times in our lives is important for us.

Once, a young man shared with me his feeling about a significant loss in his life. He said, "I didn't know that so much sadness could fit into my small body." We have all felt that way at certain times in our life. In turn, we have sought reassurance, insight, and some measure of relief.

In one of his charming Winnie the Pooh books, A. A. Milne beautifully captures how we might approach God or a close friend during such gray times. Piglet sidles up to Pooh from behind and whispers, "Pooh!"

"Yes, Piglet," Pooh answers.

"Nothing," responds Piglet, taking Pooh's paw. "I just wanted to be sure of you."

When something upsetting or sad happens, I suspect that's how most of us feel about the important people in our lives—especially God. Moreover, how such tender interactions resolve themselves can change our lives for the better, or for the worse for that matter.

There is a lot at stake during the gray periods of our lives, difficult times when we sit quietly by ourselves or reach out to others who are suffering. Sadness, and the other feelings that draw us to places we'd rather not go, can offer us new direction. When we invite meditation and prayerfulness into the troubling places in our life, suffering can actually become a window to deep inner wisdom. Unfortunately, this is not normally the case since spiritual awareness is not a natural reaction. Instead, many of us often react to emotional storms, including sadness, in several typical ways: aversion, denial, speed, aggression, and submission. Yet, when sadness or suffering is *faced directly with God*, we can change the destructive relationship we have with it. Instead, it can become an awakening, possibly even an epiphany, to enhance the next moments in our life.

Of course, this doesn't mean we don't feel the pain or should play it down. Nor should we glorify suffering to the point that we seek it out. That would be foolish. Plenty of tough times will certainly come our way of their own accord! It is just that our relationship with such experiences when they do occur offers the opportunity to experience

possibilities that weren't previously there, *if* we have the eyes
to see them.

On my first lecture tour of New Zealand in the early
1990s, I had the opportunity to drive part of the way
around the South Island with a young Catholic priest.
He had been ordained for about a year. During a lull in
the conversation, I asked him a question I like to pose to
physicians, nurses, psychotherapists, social workers, and
anyone else in the helping and healing professions who has
been out of training for about that length of time. "When
you look back on your first year's work," I asked, "is there
a particular event that stands out for you as a special teach-
able moment?"

He responded almost immediately. His eyes brightened
and his voice became animated as he shared the following
story:

> After being ordained to the priesthood for four
> months, I was called to the hospital, but due to a
> mix-up I was not told whom I was being asked to
> see. When I entered the hospital lobby, I saw a cou-
> ple sitting quietly in the corner. The man was crying
> and the woman had her head down. I walked over to
> them and introduced myself and asked if they were
> the ones who had called for me. When they both
> nodded, I asked what had happened.
>
> The woman replied (because the man was still
> unable to speak), "Father, we just gave birth to twins.

One of them was born alive but the other was born dead."

The three of us then went down the stairs to the morgue, which was in the hospital basement. When we got there, we told the attendant why we were there, and he led us over to a slab where the dead newborn was lying under a white sheet. We stood around the little shrouded form. Then, we prayed . . . and we cried.

After a while, just like a resurrection experience, we walked up the stairs to the neonatal intensive care unit to visit the other child. It was like entering a different world. Unlike the cold, silent morgue, this unit was cheerfully painted, brightly lit, and was filled with laughter, noise, and happy voices. We gazed upon the living baby lying in its incubator and we prayed again. And we cried again. But this time it was different. The tears we shed were now ones of joy.

When he looked down and paused, I quietly asked further, "Well, what lesson did you learn from this experience, Father?"

He lifted up his head, turned to me slowly, and said clearly, "I don't think I could have cried those tears of joy if I hadn't first cried those tears of deep sadness."

We have to mindfully face all of our life directly. Even the sadness. Maybe *especially* the sadness. If we do, then our relationship with our gray feelings and the rest of our lives can change. When we are totally in the present with a willingness to experience life in new ways, surprising things can happen. But, once again, as was evident in the above story, without a rich sense of prayerfulness or meditation it may well not occur. Real inner freedom and possibility dawns when we don't prejudge the next moments we face each day. When we are present, open, and willing to experience all of life as it unfolds, such a reality increasingly becomes the fabric of our daily encounters. When we aren't open, the results may be unnecessary unhappiness and missing an invitation to go deeper within ourselves. This is so with respect to serious suffering as well as in the little ups and downs of our daily life.

As Viktor Frankl, Holocaust survivor and author of *Man's Search for Meaning*, aptly noted, "To live you must choose; to love you must encounter; to grow you must suffer." Yet this doesn't happen spontaneously. Such growth during times of sadness needs to be fed by a sense of prayerfulness and meditation.

A graduate course that I led dealt to a great extent with spiritual awareness. One of the counselors attending it, in addressing the reasons how and why she was drawn to a spirit of reflection, meditation, and being in the present moment, clearly heard this message and took it to heart. She said:

> I so well remember a few years ago when I visited a Buddhist place of meditation in Washington, D.C. There was a week-long retreat taking place, and my

friend and I were allowed to join them for a few hours of sitting and walking meditation that day. I then had the unexpected opportunity to have a few moments to speak privately with the Vietnamese monk who was leading the retreat. I asked him quite bluntly: "Why do you meditate?" He answered in his almost perfect English, "I meditate to be happy. When I am in the present moment, I am happy. If I think on the past, then I am often sorry. If I think about the future, I often worry. So then I am often sorry, worry, sorry, worry, sorry, worry. But when I meditate, I am in the present, and I am happy."

The simplicity and accuracy of this simple explanation struck a deep chord in me, and I have related this story many times to friends. I am all too familiar with the "sorry-worry" obsession that plays in my head all too often. Author Eckhart Tolle expresses it so well when he writes: "Stress is caused by being 'here' but wanting to be 'there' or being in the present but wanting to be in the future. It is a split that tears you apart inside." This is one reason that prayerful meditation is a lifeline for me. It is a time for me to quietly remember to be present and, hopefully, it will spill over into the rest of my day.

No doubt we would want the same to be said of our commitment to having meditation at the core of our lives. Yet, for this to be so, we must not only have the motivation to pray; we must also employ the basic approaches to meditating in silence and solitude that have been passed down through the ages by the saints and mentors before us. Spiritual writer Jack Kornfield once said that you wouldn't go hiking in the Himalayas without a guide, so why would you want to travel the even more demanding travails of the inner life without the guidance that is available? This is particularly sensible for us to consider since we have some simple spiritual wisdom that those who have gone before us have left at our disposal to both reflect upon and use. Our only response to having such guidance need be: understand it, absorb it, and most importantly, *use it.*

Spiritual Suggestion: *Know and practice the simple, profound ways to improve your approach to meditation that have been recommended by wisdom figures through the ages.*

Meditation and contemplation together with prayer-fulness form a circle of grace that provides us with the opportunity to sense God's presence and guiding hand in our lives. As we seek to improve our sense of prayerfulness in general, we simultaneously need to attend to our formal meditation practice. This is true both in times of sadness and of joy. And so we should seek to be aware of or remind ourselves of the following simple tenets as we meditate:

- *Have a prayerful posture.* Sit or kneel, with your back straight. Look just ahead of you at something that can hold your attention (a cross, candle, etc.) as you breathe naturally and gently in the presence of God.

- *Be patient.* Rushing or expecting something only injects unnecessary pressure into your time of prayer. Be the apple slowly ripening. Don't listen, waiting for God to speak to you in some way. Quietly let the silence speak for God in new ways.

- *Don't unduly entertain, judge, or run away from your thoughts.* Just observe and let them move through you like water in a slowly running stream. To help accomplish this, you can label thoughts ("judging," "guilt," "worry," etc.) that come your way. Or use a centering word or mantra like "Lord," "love," or "gentle." You can even count your breaths, one, two, three, four. Keep counting this way until you are present to the moment again.

- *Accept where you are in prayer and don't compare.* After all, what choice do you have than to be where you are at this point? Don't waste time in favorably or unfavorably comparing your prayer life, meditation, or anything about yourself to others. Meditation and your prayer life in general is not a competition or beauty pageant.

- *Don't seek to solve anything in meditation.* Problem-solving is a good activity, but not appropriate to formal mindfulness prayer.

- *Don't expect or try to force anything.* Just relax with God; that's enough. Trust. God will do the rest.

There will be times when you are meditating that the spirit of prayer comes easily or you experience something. Other times your prayer may seem flat and empty. You may even be bored for a time.

- *Don't cling.* Just breathe in good energy and breathe out peace; then let whatever comes up flow through you like a light wind. If some issue or theme repeatedly comes up, just hand it over to God and come back to your centering word or counting your breaths again and again until you are settled. Remember, letting your meditation move with your breathing in and out is an anchor of contemplation or centering prayer.

- *Be gentle and clear with yourself.* This models how God is with you and—with God's grace—you can be this way with others too.

- *Although you should be regular in prayer, allow for times of intense, longer meditative periods.* Taking at least a few moments each day to center yourself is essential. Being disciplined to pray regularly is the spiritual backbone of a life well-lived. However, if possible, there should be times when you extend your prayer for longer periods of time.

Thomas Merton wrote a great deal about prayer and prayerfulness that reflects the above suggestions. One of his most helpful books in this regard was *New Seeds of Contemplation.* Surprisingly though, he rarely wrote about his own central approach to God when he himself sat in silence and solitude. Once, though, he was quite direct in a letter to an Eastern spiritual guide. I think he wanted to share the commonalities of their meditation approach while also indicating a key difference for himself as a Christian. Reading and quietly praying over what he wrote is a simple way to see and illustrate how one approaches God with the above tenets in mind:

> Now you ask about my method of meditation. Strictly speaking I have a very simple way of prayer. It is centered entirely on attention to the presence of God and to His will and His love. That is to say that it is centered on *faith* by which alone we can know the presence of God. One might say this gives my meditation the character described by the Prophet as "being before God as if you saw Him." Yet it does not mean imagining anything or conceiving a precise image of God, for to my mind this would be a kind of idolatry. On the contrary, it is a matter of adoring Him as invisible and infinitely beyond our comprehension, and realizing Him as all. . . . There is in my heart this great thirst to recognize totally the nothingness of all that is not God. My prayer is then a kind of praise rising out of the center of Nothing-ness and Silence. If I am still present "myself," this I recognize as an obstacle. If He wills, He can then make the Nothingness into a total clarity. If He does not will, then the Nothingness actually seems to itself to be an object and remain an obstacle. Such is

my ordinary way of prayer, or meditation. It is not "thinking about" anything, but a direct seeking of the Face of the Invisible. Which cannot be found unless we become lost in Him who is Invisible.

Befriend Anger and Other Negative Emotions

Anger can lead us to many and varied emotional and spiritual places. For instance, it may pull us back within ourselves to sit with resentment or self-blame. Or, it may guide us in another direction to face ourselves as well as the injustices in the world. In the process of a journey such as this, it can be empowering and call us to greater involvement. There are examples of this all around us as well as within our own life experiences. But, as we know, we must have the eyes to see, "eyes" that true prayerfulness can afford us.

One of the real blessings of my travels is meeting new people with wonderful backgrounds and experiences. On one of my many trips to the Midwest I had an opportunity to meet someone from an intentional lay community. He had been with the community for twenty years. During the luncheon break we had a chance to take a walk through the fields that abutted the center where the conference was being held.

After he spent a few minutes reviewing some of the comments I had made on prayerfulness during my presentation, he shared that he was having trouble with anger toward his community. He said that he didn't receive the support, encouragement, and gratitude that he felt he should get. Instead, they often ignored his needs and failed to take note of what his unique contributions were. Not only that, they seemed to be quick to affirm others who were doing a lot less than he was. The situation was brought home even more to him when he went outside the community to give a talk on social justice or to provide consultations. In those settings, he would receive wonderful accolades, something he was never given at home.

In response, I asked him, "Have they always been like this, or is this a recent change?" He responded, "No, they haven't changed. It's been like this for twenty years." Then I asked, "Well, then I am confused; why would you expect them to be different after all these years?" To which he retorted, "Well, it's just not right." (I could see his anger building.)

I then changed my tack and asked, "You have told me that outside of your lay community you have received very positive feedback. What was the feedback they gave you?" In answer to this he shared some of the gifts they affirmed. He told me how happy he was they noticed these talents. (While telling this part of the story, I noticed that his face came alive with joy.)

"Well," I reflected, "it seems that you have a situation where you don't feel appreciated within your community, and this is longstanding, but you are affirmed deeply when you minister outside it. This leaves you with a number of choices." I then smiled and said, "I could call the people in your community and tell them, 'Mend your ways!'" (He laughed and said, "Forget it! They would never listen.") Then I became serious and said, "You could also leave the community." To which he responded after a quiet moment, "No. There are also many wonderful things about these people, and I love being in this community despite all the problems I have encountered."

"That leaves us with two things that you could do. First, you could consciously absorb the positive feedback you receive elsewhere. You might consider yourself like the child with non-giving parents. 'Parental love' can come from many sources if the child has the spiritual awareness to be attentive to it. This might be true for you, too. Second, you can stop looking for the positive returns in your community, and by letting go and expecting nothing you may receive more than you think."

I could see from the expression on his face that he was pondering these things. Some time later, due to a fortuitous event that brought him to my region of the country, we had a chance to be together for a number of additional spiritual mentoring sessions. During these sessions he related how he had begun to practice meditation more deeply. In these times in silence and solitude, he was able to pick up not just what he was angry at, but also the sadness underneath the anger that stemmed from early in life when he felt misunderstood and didn't experience enough attention given to his needs and hurts. Also, he was able to begin sharpening his spiritual awareness without also sharpening his tongue or harshly judging himself or others. He became more attuned to himself and others in a way that he could now better sense others' natural limits and hurts as well as his own. He could appreciate not only his own sadness under the anger but other people's feelings as well. This made him an even better friend and community member.

Did he still get angry? Of course he did. His anger was the defensive flipside to his sense of passion. He could no more throw away his gift of passion than he could lose the defensive side to it, his anger. But he no longer castigated others. He was learning to appreciate what psychiatrist Carl Jung meant by withdrawing one's projections. Jung told his apprentices that in the second half of life, one of the greatest psychological tasks was to withdraw their projections. This is the pattern of blaming others for one's unhappiness instead of taking responsibility for it oneself. This is a spiritual principal as well, but with one additional important proviso: we do this without harsh judgment of ourselves. Instead we look at ourselves with the same love that God has for us. Once again, this is not easy and takes a commitment to practice prayerfulness as if we were always beginners. But, when we do, our negative experiences may even deepen our sense of commitment to what is good.

Anger, Injustice, and Compassion

Under the right circumstances and if it is reflected upon consciously, anger and sadness toward injustices in the world can also release great compassion in us. This was a lesson learned by the following college undergraduate student in ways that can inspire all of us to seek a greater openness to the new lessons that come from within life's darkness.

While in college, she volunteered to do "the Midnight Run." This was a program for college students to become involved in helping homeless persons in the heart of New York City. The students would gather at the school close to midnight to meet and load up vans with sandwiches they had made, as well as clothes and supplies for the homeless people they would meet later that night. They would then drive into Manhattan and stop at various well-known gathering places to meet the people they were to serve.

To do this they would stop the van and several people would come to it, calling out their needs regarding clothing. Some students would get out and hand out food and drinks. She really liked the idea of this Midnight Run, although she and her fellow students were at each stop only for a short time and she felt that the people were not able to get everything they needed.

During the first year she was involved she recalled handing out food and drink on a bitter November evening. It was not cold enough for the shelters to take everyone, but it was cold enough for the homeless to be uncomfortable. She was amazed by the number of people they had to serve. She thought to herself: "How could this many people need this much?" She felt naive and foolish at first. Although she had always been a Christian and had helped other people, she realized she was completely ignorant of the numbers of homeless people there were in New York City.

At the beginning of the second year that she was involved in this program she started the night off listening to a presentation by a guest speaker. He was the director of the program for the section of Manhattan that she and the other students often visited. He told them that he was formerly homeless himself, and that if the people they served that evening did not show them gratitude, they should not be upset. She noted that many students who were new to the program were taken aback and somewhat irritated with his statement. The director noticed this and further explained his statement. He went on to explain that he was grateful that the students were taking time to help others on a cold night when they could be sleeping. In response, many of the students smiled, but stopped when he then added, in an almost matter-of-fact way, "But that is the *least* you could do."

The smiles disappeared and a wave of silence fell over the students. He then noted that people should not have to say "thank you" for having their basic needs met. He told them that it was not fair that these people did not have enough to eat or wear, or have something simple and necessary like a shelter over their heads. He said, "We have a responsibility to them" with so much emotion that the student's eyes started to tear up. Later that night she was able to understand this sadness at an even deeper level, for as we can see in her own words, this whole experience was to profoundly change her outlook in life.

My job that evening was to work on the van distributing clothes and toiletries. We made a stop that seemed even more crowded than others. Immediately, people were screaming at once to the two of us in the back of the van, trying to get clothes and socks, knowing that we would be there for only ten minutes.

In the chaos and noise that surrounded me, in my peripheral vision I noticed a distinguished looking, older African-American man. He stood silently on the outskirts of the group, and when he caught my eye, he looked down.

I silently went over to him and asked if there was anything I could get him. He motioned me to come closer so he could share something discreetly and then whispered in my ear, "underwear," so low that I could barely hear him. I could see the discomfort in his face at having to ask a young girl no more than half his age for something so personal. In response I asked the type and size he needed and then quietly went to retrieve what he needed. It occurred to me at the very moment—and I can still feel it deeply today—the true reality of his need and the power in what was happening. I was giving this man something that he should not have had to ask for—donated underwear—and about which he felt humiliated to have to ask. I remembered what the speaker had said and my heart broke.

After leaving that man, she was changed. She became so sad and angry at the injustice of people's basic needs not being met and the extravagance of many of their neighbors—and herself—who would step over them on the street. She spoke to anyone who would listen about this shame and the needs of so many people in this country and others. This led to a decision to become a lay missionary after college. She entered the Colorado Vincentian Volunteers since it fit in well with her core beliefs about each person's intrinsic worth. She shared that "the idea of finding God working with those with less stirred me at my core. I knew that my presence alone was what God was able to use, not only to help these people, but to change me." She then went on to embrace the following quote from Vincent de Paul that explained her feelings delightfully: "If God is the center of your life, no words will be needed. Your mere presence will touch their hearts."

The way she faced her sadness and anger at injustice led her to look at and lead life in a way that was fruitful not just for herself but for others. She is a good role model for all of us when we have negative feelings and are merely tempted to waste the potential lessons from these unpleasant experiences by projecting blame onto others, seeing ourselves in a bad light, or by simply ignoring them. A more personally enriching response is instead to have a sense of intrigue about what underlies our feelings. When we personally change how we think, feel, and behave, the world can be better for it, and so can we. But for this to happen, having a *prayerful attitude* is not just beneficial . . . it is essential.

Spiritual Suggestion: *Appreciate the Elements of an Attitude of Prayerfulness.*

There are certain questions that are at the heart of the journey of prayerfulness—especially when experiencing and seeking to spiritually profit from negative experiences like anger. Some are general questions such as:

- What attitudes must we unpack for the inner journey so we can learn rather than simply condemn ourselves or project all the blame on others?
- What are the particular perils to consider when anger or other negative emotions call us to travel more deeply in the spiritual life?

More specifically, are we courageous enough to learn the most from our strong negative emotions? This happens when we become:

- humble enough to see our growing edges as persons without simultaneously letting this awareness blind us to the talents and gifts we also have been given;
- in tune with the emotions and the thoughts and beliefs that have produced them;
- persons with values and convictions yet who are not closed-minded;
- individuals with self-respect but who can admit the need to change personally and grow;
- accepting of criticism and interested in a more complete self-awareness (including knowledge of

> our many faults and shortcomings) without falling prey to self-condemnation;
>
> - understanding of the role others may play in influencing us in the wrong way, but not resorting to the very dangerous defense of projecting the blame onto others for the difficulties we are experiencing.

When we are upset, it is hard to move from an angry reaction to reflection. As a matter of fact, sometimes it is even harder to realize that in the first place we are reacting in an angry way! In such instances, we may not see our anger. We may instead express our anger indirectly by being an obstructionist or by withdrawing. This is called passive-aggressive behavior. On the other hand, we may not even realize that we are angry inside since our public faces are chronically nice.

When this occurs, we are living dishonestly, not prayerfully. The result is to lose an opportunity to be aware of, and also prevent, undercutting the people with whom we are angry. We also lose an opportunity to limit the unnecessary suffering we are experiencing within—something that can, over a period of time, actually cause physical problems (referred to as psycho-physical disorders) as well as spiritual ones.

Prayerfulness, on the other hand, calls us to meet anger by taking a step back, looking at our emotions and the thoughts and beliefs producing them with a sense of intrigue instead of blame for others or ourselves. In this way, when we examine our anger, we can do so in ways that help us to learn more deeply about our past patterns and therefore become freer to deal with actual injustices in the most effective way possible.

With this in mind, here are some final questions we can ask ourselves, especially with respect to experiencing and owning our anger. They are intended to help remove the danger of projection in order to better understand what is going on within us.

- What did I get angry at today? (Not, what made me angry?)
- With whom did I get angry today? (Not, who made me angry?)
- As well as the reasons apparent to me now for my being angry or annoyed, what else might be responsible for this anger or the intensity of my reaction?
- How did I deal with my anger? Did I conceal, deny, or ignore it? Did I play it down or cover it up? (Don't get me wrong, he is not a bad person, just a very misguided one.)
- Did I spontaneously allow my anger to rise and come to the surface in a healthy way?
- Was I able to review my anger and try to constructively deal with disagreements, with the understanding that communication won't solve everything, but that opening up a discussion about our differences is certainly a start? Or, did I just try to scare people off with my anger?

- Did I present my anger to the source that precipitated it, or did I put the anger on someone else or make believe I wasn't angry?

Spiritual mindfulness is ideally suited to facing anger and all of our negative emotions. Once again, real spirituality dawns when God becomes as real as the problems and joys we face each day. We grow and deepen when we seek, with a sense of intrigue, to fathom new knowledge about ourselves at times when we feel upset and vulnerable. It is a shame to waste these opportunities by running away or becoming defensive. If we remain defensive, nothing will change in us even when God is giving us the opportunity to become freer and to see how humility can teach us to be strong. In line with this is the Franciscan theme: there is nothing so strong as true gentleness and nothing so gentle as true strength.

Honor "Unofficial Retreats"

Thomas Merton once noted that illnesses can be opportunities to quiet ourselves down, let go of the world's demands, and open ourselves to some unexpected time alone with God. This can be seen quite well in the following example of a counselor who, though quite healthy, had some unexpected experiences with physical limitation.

A fall had disabled her. Fortunately, it came after a spiritual experience that changed her life in a significant way. She knew that if the accident had happened before this sense of conversion, she probably would have emotionally shut down. However, her spiritual awakening had given her hope and a profound feeling that she was not alone. She trusted that God would give her what she needed to handle her hardships. But she had also come to understand that God didn't make her problems go away. Rather she was discovering that God would give her the strength to persevere and let those very difficulties transform her. In her own words:

After I left the hospital, each day was a series of new steps. After two days I could make it to the bathroom with a walker. After two weeks I could walk without assistance. I went back to work after only a month. After four months I went on my first hike.

This hike was a huge step for her but came with a hidden cost. Ten days later, she developed Lyme disease from a tick bite during this excursion into the woods. She was to learn yet another lesson from this unfortunate event.

Once the Lyme disease hit, I was drained of my remaining physical and mental strength. I was so exhausted that I saw only one choice—I needed to quit my job. But who would I be if I was not working? My work defined me. What could I do if I was not working? My answer came after my first week as an unemployed person: I would heal. I suffered emotional and physical pain for over ten years but never took a break to heal. Not once. It was finally my time to be healed, and I had the resources and support to do it.

Looking back at this turning point in my life, I realized that not only did I need to heal, I also needed to develop better coping skills and healthier ways of looking at the world. During my time at home, I began learning to focus on my priorities, still myself, listen to God, and be present. I still remember the first Monday when I did not have to go to work. I had the idea to cut up a fresh pineapple for breakfast.

But then out of habit I thought to myself, "I don't have time for that." I had to catch myself and realize that I *did* have time to cut up fruit. I could cut up fruit all day if I wanted to! I could even go for a leisurely walk, learn to play the piano, or read a good book. The possibilities seemed endless.

As the weeks went by and she began to slow down, she started noticing things around her that she never noticed before when she was rushing through life. For example, she began to experience the joy of solitude. She had so much time to herself: to think, to listen, to be present! She began to find new "companions" on her journey—the little black-and-white ducks who dive in the water at her favorite walking spot, the beautiful sound of Beethoven's piano sonatas, and the colorful characters of Dickens's novels. She often joked that she was on an eight-hour silent retreat every day. She spoke little from the time she woke up until her husband came home from work. In this unexpected and imposed time out (because she viewed her situation as an "unofficial retreat" rather than a period of inactivity to be railed against), she was able to welcome new, positive moments of prayer that may not have taken if all had remained "well" in her life. She was also able in this time to become even more sensitive to the prayerfulness that was already there in her life.

This, of course, should be a primary goal for all of us. When we see what a flourishing sense of spiritual mindfulness looks like, our desire to seek to be prayerfully attuned to living differently is reinforced. We are also able to recognize more clearly when we are not living with prayerfulness. Prayerfulness has many dimensions and varies for each of us in our own situations. Let's take a few moments to reflect on that now.

Spiritual Suggestion: *Be sensitive to the positive moments of prayerfulness.*

When we seek to develop an attitude of prayerfulness, we are better able to navigate the perils of spiritual intimacy. The following suggestions offer specific examples of what forms prayerfulness can take in our lives. Noting and reflecting on these forms can give us the passion and faithfulness we need to practice them. Stop and linger on ones that particularly strike you as relevant.

Illustrations of Positive Movements of Prayerfulness in Your Life

- Peace, joy, understanding, and patience spontaneously begin to take the place of anger, resentment, and other negative emotions.
- When someone misbehaves rather than merely reacting, we reflect and act in a helpful way.
- Judging ourselves or others is frequently replaced by a helpful compassion that can lead to positive change.

- Crippling guilt, which pulls us into the past and leaves us there, diminishes; we become aware of our faults, but in a way that makes the present and future different.
- We recognize when we have become inordinately preoccupied with the future, and a greater appreciation of the present moment and the ability to stay in that moment develops.
- A more natural tendency to move away from useless worry takes root in us. In its place we meet life's demands more often with a concern that involves recognizing the challenges, appreciating their source, planning what we can do, doing it, and then letting God take care of the rest.
- Our awareness of ourselves and those around us is more frequently marked by acceptance, compassion, and understanding.
- A deeper appreciation for patience and vulnerability instead of a desire to control becomes evident.
- Surprising episodes of gratitude for people and things we used to take for granted show themselves more readily in our daily encounters.
- There is less interest in competition, less concern about what others may think of us.
- Experiences of collaboration and connectedness seem to spontaneously occur.
- A real sense of intrigue about our own thoughts, ways of understanding, perceptions, emotions, and

behaviors begins to replace the old tendency toward self-blame, resentment, or fear.

- We don't automatically believe our thoughts—especially the negative ones—without checking them out.
- Self-awareness becomes more a gentle process of self-appreciation rather than a process of comparison of ourselves with others.
- We seek to be more inclusive rather than exclusive in the way we bring everything into our prayers and lives.
- A desire increases in us to use our speech to benefit others by being truthful, expressive of our own experiences, sensitive to the feelings of others, supportive, encouraging, accurate, and specific rather than vague, negative, and self-referential in an exaggerated way.

When we experience these positive movements in prayerfulness, we discover why and how making God part of our entire day, not just part of our prayer time, results in a more centered, full, and compassionate way of life. Surely, aspiring to live in such a wonderful way is a noble and rewarding goal.

Appreciate Inner Companions in Hope

I n the book *Tuesdays with Morrie*, one of the many delightful interchanges between sportswriter Mitch Albom and his dying mentor Morrie is the following one:

Okay, question, I say to Morrie. His bony fingers hold glasses across his chest, which rises and falls with each labored breath.

"What's the question?" he says.

Remember the Book of Job?

"From the Bible?"

Right. Job is a good man, but God makes him suffer. To test his faith.

"I remember."

Takes away everything he has, his house, his money, his family . . .

"His health."

Makes him sick.

"To test his faith."

Right. To test his faith. So, I'm wondering . . .

"What are you wondering?"

What you think about that?

Morrie coughs violently. His hands quiver as he drops them by his side.

"I think," he says, smiling, "God overdid it."

I am sure many of us have felt like Morrie at times—especially when things became very dark for us. Sometimes in our life we have or must face unexpected trauma. By definition, such an experience is overwhelming, disorienting, and opens up so many questions in life. The natural response is to ask, "Why?" Yet, until we can let go of this question and find new ways of relating to God and the event, moving on and moving deeper in our life is almost impossible. One of the ways we accomplish this is to appreciate our companions of hope. Mitch thought he was going to be Morrie's companion, and he was, but in the end it was Morrie who became the unexpected companion of hope for Mitch. The following story (taken from my book *Crossing the Desert*) by a sensitive and deep young woman is a poignant illustration of another companion in hope:

> Through the years many companions have blessed me on my journey by imparting wisdom and lightening my load. My two-year-old niece was one of these surprising companions.
>
> I had just graduated from high school and was preparing to spend most of the next month in or near the hospital. I would be undergoing corrective facial surgery that was considered quite dangerous, so naturally I was quite anxious about it.

My niece, Shelly, had crawled into my suitcase because she wanted to go with me. She looked up and saw me crying as I was packing because I did not want to face what was ahead of me. When she saw this she looked straight into my eyes and said, "Don't cry. Jesus make it all better."

I was so caught up in my own preoccupations that I didn't pay much attention to this tiny angel's kind words. In a few hours, I left for the airport. Little did I realize that in a few short days, both of our lives would hang in the balance and be changed forever.

After the surgery, I experienced several serious complications. It was so bad that the staff prepared my family for the possibility that I might not make it through the night. While my sisters were on the phone together speaking and worrying about me, my niece Shelly unlatched the back door, went into the back yard, and fell into the swimming pool. Although she was gone but for a short while before her mother realized the silence in the house and her absence, it was long enough for her to have her little lungs fill with water and drown.

Shelly died that night and I lived. I struggled with this for the longest time. I blamed myself and wallowed in self-pity. As Pema Chodron says in her book *When Things Fall Apart*, "We usually don't see pain as a source of potential wisdom. When something is painful, we want to rid ourselves of the feeling as soon as possible, and we even cultivate a subtle aggression against ourselves." That description fit me exactly.

I wanted to rid myself of these feelings as soon as possible. I spent considerable time in prayer and meditation as well as in counseling, searching for a way to reconcile why I was here and she was gone. The person I least expected to die, died. The person I anticipated might die—me—survived. It was inconceivable to me. All my assumptions were challenged.

However, the experience eventually did give me a new perspective. As in the case of all people who are eventually able to surface from trauma, I let go of why it had to happen. Instead, the search for an answer eventually led me to a different place: the valuing of being in the present moment. There are no guarantees. All we have is this moment. There may not be a tomorrow. Those moments with Shelly were our last together on this earth. I realized I could take nothing for granted.

It's strange how we learn as children to believe life is fair. We make sure everyone has the same number of cookies. Everyone gets a ride on the pony. Then we grow up and discover, life is many things—but fair is not one of them.

I clung to Shelly's last words to me, "Jesus make it all better." I realized I had to trust God in this. If I did, I knew I could then choose to move out of the darkness and continue living my life—but in a different, more enlightened, way. I would take the lesson Shelly had taught me and move ahead as best as I could. I would also remember and take deeply to heart what one of my professors had taught me: "If we remain sensitive to the presence of God in faith and in prayer, and in the darkness of confusion and suffering, the darkness will teach us, it will become new light."

From the insights the young woman above was able to absorb from her experience of trauma and loss, we can feel the fruits of her developing sense of spiritual mindfulness about life, *her* life. Her reflective prayerfulness did not keep her from the terrible realities she had to face, but it permitted her to see that it is not the amount of darkness in the world that matters. It is not even the amount of darkness in herself that matters. It is how she stood in that darkness that made the difference in how she would live the rest of her life. Shelly was her inner companion on this journey.

In C. S. Lewis's book, *The Lion, the Witch, and the Wardrobe*, we see the youngest girl, Lucy, entering a large closet in a game of hide-and-seek. She finds what she expects—coats, hats, mufflers, and sweaters. But then she goes in deeper, and she is eventually led out into a new and very different world. And there she meets a new companion and guide to this strange new world, a faun named Mr. Tumnus. When we prayerfully enter our own darkness and sadness with our eyes open to see God in new ways, the same can be true for us. We, too, can find what we expect but possibly something more as well. But it takes a willingness to eventually let go of "the whys" of what has happened to us so we can live with the questions in new ways rather than merely seeking to be rescued by pat answers where there are none—at least for now.

In Ephesians, Chapter 6, the call to "be strong in the Lord and in his mighty power. . . . [So] that when the day of evil comes, you may be able to stand your ground" is clearly set out (Eph 6:10–13). However, even when terrible things eventually open up new spiritual opportunities, as we have seen in the above story and possibly in our own lives, we know a terrible event will first cause great distress and doubt. Prayerfulness doesn't remove this as we move toward meeting God and our own inner faith and strength in new ways. Instead, it opens us up to see God helping us chart our evolving spiritual life in a way that both the journey and destination are life-giving at the very time we need such a helpful navigator in our lives.

We can see this in a very unique and marked way in the following experience of another woman's own poignant prayer process when she was faced with a complex family tragedy:

> Ephesians 6 became all the more real to me when I wrestled with the death of my brother, age eleven. Aside from the personal loss of my sibling, I watched as my parents' shaky marriage and my mother's already unstable mental health worsened. Both, of

course, resulted in increased dysfunction for the whole family. For the first time of which I am aware, I turned from my simplistic understanding that God was in authority and my role was unquestioning obedience. I faced my Creator and demanded an answer to "Why?" Reflecting now, I realize that this was an important beginning to a fuller spiritual formation, but that it was only the beginning. I felt as one with Metropolitan Anthony of Sourozh, who asked, "How dare God be blissful, how dare He be so comfortable when *I* am in trouble?"

Over the course of my middle school years, I began to journal my thoughts and write out my prayers to God. A new theme emerged, in the form of a new question: "If God was there watching my family, and if he was allowing the suffering I was experiencing, could he still be good?" Once I was able to answer that question—and know that I might not like what God was allowing, but that that did not necessarily preclude his nature from being good—I realized that I had a choice. I could either seek to identify God's plan for my life through continuing to pursue a relationship with him, or I could try to walk away from him spiritually. The former seemed the better option, since the decline of the relationship with my parents made God the one Parent with whom I was still in regular, healthy contact.

I hoped one day to understand my present situation, looking back, but in the meantime, I at least felt the reassurance of God's presence. I was coming to own the advice of Rilke in his *Letters to a Young Poet*: "Do not search now for answers which cannot be given you because you could not live them. It is a matter of living everything. Live the questions now. Perhaps you will then gradually, without noticing it, one day live right into the answer."

I became satisfied, not because I had found the answers to my "whys," but because I had become more secure that the Keeper of those answers was strengthening me to face what was unknown or seemingly unreasonable and to stand firm because of my identity before God and the scriptural assurances of God's love for me.

In facing trauma and sadness, people who hold on to "the why has this happened to me" question have great difficulty letting go and advancing. It's similar for people who move through life expecting justice. They become disillusioned, whereas those who reach for love and are open to see it and God's presence in new ways amidst the very evil or trauma they are experiencing turn to live in the face of it in new ways. They discover hope as their inner companion and know that just as some others who have been traumatized can be transformed into especially compassionate souls, they, too, can face injustice with newfound strength if they are open to hearing God's surprising voice.

Jack Nelson once said that while he was encountering the suffering of the poor while walking the streets of Calcutta, he started to scream at God. Then, during his lament, with his eyes prayerfully opened, all of a sudden he realized that in the suffering of the poor, God was screaming at *him*.

After a traumatic incident, the whole world may seem dark or, at the very least, gray. Yet, what can come to the fore with the spiritual awareness with which prayerfulness graces us is that suffering need not be the whole story if we have the eyes to see. But sometimes, as in the following story, someone near to us may need to have those eyes for us.

Once, a young Catholic nun was deep in depression after fully realizing elements of a devastating past that had long simmered below her level of consciousness. She felt crippled, but kept it to herself, except for her closest friend and her therapist. Finally, she did share with another of her friends how psychologically crippled she felt. She even reported that going to morning prayer with the other Sisters was done for no other reason than to avoid them asking if something was wrong.

In response, the friend looked at her, smiled, and said to her surprise, "How wonderful it is that you have the courage, inner strength, and fortitude to get up and go down to pray. It doesn't matter what reason you give yourself for it. It is something that you are able to accomplish even though you are depressed. It is an anchor to hold on to at this point and to build from while taking care of and nurturing yourself as you move through this terrible darkness."

Although her friend's statement didn't immediately generate a major change, it gave her another way to look at her behavior. It was a point of light in the darkness. It also demonstrated that one of her inner companions that she was unable to recognize was courage. It was a quiet strength that she eventually was able to unwrap with some help from others.

The following story is told by someone who had experienced a tragic attack by someone she trusted when she was very young. The events described in this account took place in her later teen years. It is an amazing account of courage and survival, all the more so because it demonstrates how life cannot be destroyed. Her accomplishments are even more amazing, given the trauma she had to deal with in the early formative years of her life.

> I was seventeen years old when I did a transatlantic crossing, from Maine to Ireland, in a thirty-eight-foot sailboat. There were four of us who sailed: me, my father, the owner of the boat, and his daughter. This experience taught me the truism of challenges as opportunities for growth! For instance, on day sixteen, we realized we had fallen off course. We were being pushed farther north by the wind and the current. This meant we were sailing in choppier and colder water than we had intended. The waves were steeper, and the boat pounded hard into the wind.
>
> After days of these conditions, the boat began to groan and shudder. Water began to leak into the

cabin. Our sleeping quarters became damp. The other two crew members developed frostbitten feet. The mainsail tore. We were all sleep deprived, cold, and wet.

In spite of this extreme discomfort, I found the experience of being at the helm at night to be exhilarating. I was thrilled by the power of the waves as they rose up, high as mountains on either side of the boat, and the way they surged us forward with tremendous force. Water spilled into the back and sides of the cockpit, and around my boots. I was alone in a sea of swirling phosphorus. It was as if the sky had fallen and I was sailing alone across the galaxy. The glittering light in the cold dark waters was our only source of light, as the gray weather blended into night without change for days and days.

The crossing took twenty-eight days; the first hint of land far off in the horizon was an incredible moment. I felt like a true warrior, hero, and, definitely, a survivor!

I knew this woman personally. I met her later in her life—long after her abuse—and she continues to be an inspiration, a warrior, hero, and definitely a survivor to me. I may never be as strong as she is or be able to take on the challenges she has had to face, but I do take strength from her as I hope others can take strength from me in small ways at times.

As I spoke about this voyage with her and what she could now see about herself, I began to appreciate from her responses, and ones from persons like her, some of the fruits of prayerfulness when we have the courage to face life completely and openly with God. To see such fruits can be a true encouragement for us, particularly at a time when we are lost and have few goals for ourselves. And so, taking a few moments of silence to reflect over the fruits of prayerfulness at this juncture, as well as in the future, may well be a worthwhile step.

Spiritual Suggestion: *Recognize and recall each day the fruits of prayerfulness in your life.*

When we are suffering or our lives seem dark, prayerfulness helps us to be more in tune with what life has to teach us, sometimes in new, transforming ways. When our emotional and spiritual place is in "the now," our eyes are wide open to the dynamic presence of the Holy Spirit. Prayerfulness can:

- lift us out of stagnant, obsessive thought patterns;
- alert us to when we are not living the experience of life but merely wandering around in an envelope of thought, thinking we are alive;
- move us out of the thicket of preoccupations, fears, anxieties, and worries about the past or future by having us "simply" be where we are;

- help us appreciate that *all* things/people/situations change;
- give us the space to step back and get unglued from our desires, demands, and attachments so we can have the freedom to flow with what is;
- enable us to get in touch with the invisible bonds of shame, loneliness, secrets, addictions, hopes, and other places in our hearts where we have expended a great deal of energy in avoidance;
- help us forgo the comfort of denial and avoidance for the peace that allows us to fear nothing but instead welcome all of our emotions, cognitions (ways of thinking, perceiving, and understanding), and impulses with compassion and clarity;
- open up true space for others by opening it up in ourselves;
- help us imitate Jesus and others we admire by reaching out to others who are in need;
- enable us to see our defenses, failures, and growing edges as opportunities for new wisdom and openings to life (because rather than judging, we are intrigued by them);
- ask us if we are relating to ourselves with kindness and clarity;
- awaken us to our habitual, possibly deadening styles of thinking, believing, and behaving;
- allow us especially to become freer by taking "the sacred pause" spiritual guide Tara Brach suggests when confronted with suffering (this pause is made

up of a desire to recognize what is happening, allowing it, and experiencing it rather than trying to just figure out or control it);

- help us see that permanent problems are so because of the way we formulate them, thus teaching us that loosening our grip on such ways of seeing our world makes all the difference;

- set aside the way we have created meaning so all things can be made new;

- increase our appreciation of how little things can produce emotional peaks and valleys in our lives;

- develop our respect for both formal prayer (meditation) and informal approaches (prayerfulness or spiritual mindfulness) that increase our awareness of "the now" during the day;

- incorporate simple practices, such as taking a few moments to notice something enjoyable; appreciating our own small, beautiful acts; and slowing down when we are caught up in a sense of mindless, driven action;

- encourage us to wonder more about what thoughts, emotions, and events help us create peace rather than suffering;

- teach us that being spiritually aware is more natural when we don't seek it aggressively, or with expectations or fear that it won't produce dramatic results;

- have us welcome and learn from, rather than label and reject, so-called negative experiences such as boredom;

- help us be clear and sort things out as well as deepen ourselves;
- encourage humility, help us see our foibles, and over time increase the enjoyment we have in being with ourselves and alone with God;
- result in less dependence on reinforcement by others while at the same time setting the stage for taking a healthier part in community;
- protect our inner fire by helping us see when we need to withdraw for time alone and also uncover time within our daily activity where we can take a few breaths and center ourselves, rather than be disturbed that we are being delayed or postponed in our travels or activities;
- make us more in tune with the voice of God that is continually being drowned out by society and our own inner habitual voices.

Slowly reflecting on the above fruits can help us to better notice and more fully embrace them. If you are like me, when awareness of them is forgotten, there is a tendency to move through life like a driver on a long journey who realizes upon his arrival that he has little sense of the roads he has traveled. During the stresses of life, especially when we are suffering in some way, not being spiritually mindful would be a real shame, given the need we have for such support to continue our journey with God in the most alive way possible.

If we wish to be truly prayerful, we must seek to do whatever we can to enhance our being in the now—with our eyes wide open to the presence of God in unfamiliar ways that we have neither expected nor hoped for. Such is the very process of discovery into which prayerfulness can lead us.

TWO

Discovering the Peace,
Uncovering the Joy

Taking the Next Step
in the Spiritual Life

Making a decision is only the beginning of
things. When someone makes a decision, he is
really diving into a strong current that will carry
him to places he had never dreamed of when he
first made that decision.

—Paulo Coelho
The Alchemist

A Month of Quotes, Questions, and Spiritual Themes

A Personal Retreat on Prayer and Prayerfulness

Up to this point, this book has sought to raise your sense of prayerfulness (what some people term spiritual mindfulness or awareness) to improve the navigation of the real perils involved in spiritual intimacy. One spiritual guide summed up the dangers all of us face when we want to live a spiritually involved life by cautioning that an involved Christian "travels a narrow and winding road between banality and crucifixion." However, there is so much more to the Christian journey than dangers. As we can see from the lives of holy people, the movement with and toward God also involves deep peace and joy. And so, taking the next step in the interior life requires us to be mindful of all that the spiritual journey involves.

A sense of mindfulness like this merits taking out at least a little quiet time each day to center ourselves on a theme, which will help us to be mindful as we move through our day. The amount of time for such a "personal retreat" can be as little as two or three minutes. More important than the actual time is the *regularity* of our practice so a new rhythm can take place in our lives.

As in any exercise to seed greater spiritual awareness, following a few steps can provide enough discipline to structure this personal month-long retreat. Though you don't have to leave home for this retreat, it still allows you to find a focus in your life that is both intentional and renewing. The simple discipline, which is familiar to many, is:

- Find a place of quiet in the morning.
- Center yourself by sitting or kneeling up straight.
- Look forward a few feet in front of you so as not to get distracted, while breathing in spiritual energy and joy and breathing out inner peace.
- After two or three minutes of silence, read the quotes, question, or theme provided for that day and pick a word from it that will form a "spiritual nest" to which you can return for a few seconds at different points in your day.
- Finally, at the end of the day, as you go to bed, take the word with you as a mantra for a few moments as you fall asleep.

Don't "overthink" the day's theme. Instead let it act as an inner church into which you can enter with openness, intrigue, acceptance, and gentleness. If you find yourself getting caught in thought or undue concern about the reflection you have read, then return to the words Jesus gave to you through his disciples in the fifteenth chapter of John's Gospel: "You are my friends" (Jn 15:14).

A retreat is a time to move closer to a loving God to gain greater clarity and spiritual intimacy so you can in turn offer it to others. On the one hand, if you forget the friendship of God, you may anxiously vacillate between self-indictment and resentment. Or you may blame others. On the other hand, if you forget that spiritual clarity is a goal, then you may neglect to bring the lessons you receive home to yourself so you can face your growing edges and sins directly. Therefore, during your personal retreat the balance between *both* kindness and clarity is crucial.

Each day, please prepare yourself as described above and begin.

DAY 1
Faithfulness in Prayer

Being faithful to taking out time in silence and solitude with God is one of the most important elements of the spiritual life. Yet, we often have a sense of resistance to it. In the following section from *The Genesee Diary*, Henri Nouwen receives guidance from his spiritual director, Abbot John Eudes Bamberger:

"In the beginning," John Eudes said, "your thoughts will wander, but after a while you will discover that it becomes easier to stay quietly in the presence of the Lord. If your head seems filled with worries or concerns, you might like to start with some psalms or a Scripture reading that can help you to concentrate and then you will be better prepared for silent meditation. When you are faithful in this, you will slowly experience yourself in a deeper way. Because in this useless hour in which you do nothing 'important' or 'urgent,' you have to come to terms with your basic powerlessness, and have to feel your fundamental inability to solve your or other people's problems or to change the world. When you do not avoid that experience, obligations become less urgent, crucial, and important and lose their power over you. They will leave you free during your time with God and take their appropriate place in your life."

Henri Nouwen's honest response to this advice was, "It seems very convincing to me, even obvious. The only task left is this: simply doing it in obedience."

The question that remains for each us as well is: what will it take for us to establish and be faithful to time alone with God in silence and solitude—even if it be only a few minutes in the beginning of our day?

Follow Abbot John Eudes's advice, or simply choose a word (Lord, Spirit, gentleness . . .) that is important and nurturing to you and sit with it quietly for a few moments. Let this ritual help start each day for you.

DAY 2
Spiritual Mindfulness

Remaining prayerful can be transformative. Jesus advises us to be like little children. In this regard, we have good role models for being in the now with a sense of gratitude rather than being preoccupied with the future—a future that may never happen, for that matter. As Jerry Braza recognizes in his book *Moment by Moment*:

> Mindfulness is a natural state of living moment by moment. Observe young children, and you will quickly notice that the majority of their awareness is in the present moment. . . . I recall a time driving my young children somewhere when we approached a railroad crossing as the lights began to flash and the safety gate went down. My first thought was "Oh no! We're going to be held up by a train and be late." Just then, my daughter called out from the backseat, "Daddy, Daddy, we're so lucky! We get to watch the train go by!" Her awareness of the present moment was a wonderful reminder to stop and enjoy what the journey had to offer along the way.

In the above story we can see the importance of paying attention to where you are and what you are doing. Often "the now" is filled with many wonderful gifts *if we have the eyes to see*. As you move through the rest of this day, catch yourself when you are becoming preoccupied with the future and lean back into the now. Experience it and what God is teaching you about yourself and spiritual intimacy.

DAY 3
Nonjudgmental Reception in Meditation and Prayerfulness

In a presentation at Harvard, Mark Epstein noted that one of the goals of meditation is to stop our egos from obstructing the fluency of the material coming. He noted that according to John Cage, when sound and other stimuli come into our meditation period, the mind often shows off trying to identify them. The art rather than the science of meditation brings your mind to a less complicated place. You experience everything in prayer without unconsciously or consciously grasping certain experiences and pushing others away.

In today's meditation and during the day as you seek to be spiritually mindful or prayerful, catch yourself judging, classifying, rejecting, or admiring someone—what they are saying or your thoughts about them—and seek instead to just take in the information, observing without judgment, and see where it takes you.

DAY 4
Our Precious Breath

There is a sign as you enter the place where the Vietnamese monk and spiritual guide Thich Nhat Hanh lives. It says: "You have arrived. Enjoy breathing."

This may sound silly since you probably don't seem to pay much attention to your breath. But stop breathing for a minute and you will see how sacred breath is! Why not practice conscious breathing several times during the day? Stop what you are doing, and in a natural way breathe in energy and passion and breathe out a sense of peace. Breaking up your day this way by being more conscious of your breath can help you re-create a life worth living and slow you down. Surprisingly, it can make you not only more mindful, but also more productive. Such mindfulness can break the pattern of simply rushing through things toward the grave.

DAY 5
Gratitude and Perspective

Gratitude feeds a healthy perspective. In turn, a healthy perspective allows you to see the world with a greater sense of gratitude. Gratitude and perspective form a circle of grace. You can get into the circle through either of the two entry ways: you can look with grateful eyes or can seek to put things in perspective. Whichever way you choose puts you in touch with a greater reality. The following comment by Thich Nhat Hanh, who experienced so much suffering during the Vietnam War and later in his work with children haunted and physically wounded by the napalm attacks in their country, offers a good example:

> Life is filled with suffering, but it is also filled with many wonders, like the blue sky, the sunshine, the eyes of a baby. To suffer is not enough. We must also be in touch with the wonders of life. They are within us and all around us, everywhere, any time.

Some people faced with suffering feel that being grateful is naive, not practical. Yet, if you believe that God is gifting you at every point in your life with something as yet undiscovered, is it practical not to recognize it? Look with gratitude for the familiar things and people in your life today, whether it be a morning cup of coffee or the smile of your spouse or a friend. Be open to the unfamiliar or what you might normally step away from or around to see what is there as well.

DAY 6
The Freedom of Meditation and Prayerfulness

Look for areas of your life that are noncompetitive, nongrasping, and not worrisome but instead are filled with freedom, peace, fun, and joy. The positive psychology movement might call these "flow." These areas give you some indication of what meditation and prayerfulness are like. When you sit down to pray, lean back into the now and be reflective. Slow down your day and fully live the time you have on earth. Then you are entering one of those places in your life that provides space.

Clark Strand in his simple, enchanting book The *Wooden Bowl* puts it this way:

> Perhaps you have had the experience of waking well-rested on a Saturday morning. Your mind is alert, but you have not yet begun to think about the day. The sun is shining in the yard, and all around you is perfectly clear morning light. That alertness sustains itself without even trying. You may not even notice it except for the feeling of being rested and ready for the day.
>
> The experience of meditation is something like that. When you meditate you are not trying to have any particular experience. You are simply awake. . . . It feels a little like having enough space to think, enough room to move and breathe, or simply "be." . . . Once you realize how simple meditation is, you will know how often we forget to be simple, and what a funny thing that is.

When you sit down to meditate, take a few deep breaths. Smile at your life and what God has given you. Enter into meditation as an alert, fresh space. This is a good image to bring to mind and let God meet you in new, refreshing ways.

DAY 7
Patience

There is a tendency to want to advance faster in prayer and prayerfulness than we are capable of at the time. This was true in the desert in the fourth century just as it is in modern society. Knowing this, Abba Macarius once said:

> Don't try to understand everything. Take on board as much as you can and try to make it work for you. Then the things that are hidden will be made clear to you.

During the day seek to be intrigued about all that you experience in prayer and life. Don't try to understand, control, judge, or compare. Simply experience it. There will be time later to reflect in a critical way on it. In this way you will see and hear so much more than you ever expected.

DAY 8
Our Life as Pilgrimage

When pulled into the many details of daily life, it is easy to forget that life is a pilgrimage. In *The Art of Pilgrimage* Phil Cousineau wrote, "Making a pilgrimage is a way to prove your faith and find answers to your deepest problems." His comment also shows why prayerfulness is so important. It is the process of unfolding your "spiritual map" of the interpersonal and natural geography. Maps are so important when we feel lost or lonely, when everything seems dark. Cousineau writes:

> Centuries of travel lore suggest that when we no longer know where to turn, our real journey has just begun . . . that [this experience] will stir our heart and restore our sense of wonder. It is down the path to the deeply real where time stops and we are seized by the mysteries. This is the journey we cannot not take.

To this, Kyriacos Markides—author of several books on Christian mysticism—responds in his book *Gifts of the Desert*: "The purpose of pilgrimages is primarily to create conditions within ourselves that will make us receptive to the light, to the energies of the Holy Spirit."

Questions worth pondering: How might you see each of your days on this earth as a pilgrimage? Wouldn't it be an inducement to be more spiritually mindful if you did see each of your days that way?

DAY 9
Clarity

When you are spiritually mindful, you begin to have the freedom to notice your emotions without judgment. You become intrigued by your anger, grasping, fears, and aversions. This allows you to explore them further without picking on yourself or blaming others for your negative experiences. This new way of viewing yourself and the world actually detoxifies you. In *One Minute Wisdom*, Anthony de Mello offers this dialogue between a spiritual master and his disciple:

> "Why do I fail to find God?"
> "Why does the drunkard fail to see his home? Find out what it is that makes you drunk. To see you must be sober."

What are the things in your life that seem to prevent you from being free enough to experience life and God in new ways? Or, using the metaphor from the above story, what makes you "drunk" at this point in your life's journey?

DAY 10
Relationship

When you are spiritually mindful, your relationships with others and God are closely interrelated. When God gave Moses the Ten Commandments he was in effect telling the Israelites that they must not only find God vertically in prayer (Commandments 1–3), but also horizontally through each other (Commandments 4–10), This is necessary today as well. This sounds attractive, but as Metropolitan Anthony of Sourozh (Anthony Bloom) pointed out in his classic work *Beginning to Pray*, in reality it is often quite difficult.

So often when we say "I love you" we say it with a huge "I" and a small "you." We use love as a conjunction instead of it being a verb implying action. It's no good just gazing out into open space hoping to see the Lord; instead we have to look closely at our neighbour, someone whom God has willed into existence, someone whom God has died for. Everyone we meet has a right to exist, because he has value to himself, and we are not used to this. The acceptance of otherness is a danger to us, it threatens us. . . . Love is difficult. Christ was crucified because he taught a kind of love which is a terror for men, a love which demands total surrender: it spells death. . . .

To meet God means to enter into the "cave of the tiger"—it is not a pussy cat you meet—it's a tiger. The realm of God is dangerous. You must enter into it and not just seek information about it.

Maximos (Kyriacos Markides), the Greek Orthodox bishop of Cyprus, puts it this way:

You can develop the capacity to commune with God, and as a result of that you learn to commune with your fellow human beings. Once you do that you can never again experience loneliness or anxiety or the feeling of being lost.

What can you do today that will help you to speak and act toward others in ways that will increase rather than diminish their happiness and peace?

DAY 11
Everything Is Sacred

One of the "products" of prayerfulness is a recognition of the sacredness all around you. It is more than what you experience in church or religious rituals. William James, the father of American psychology and a physician, in has groundbreaking book *Pragmatism*, noted:

> To anyone who has ever looked on the face of a dead child or parent, the mere fact that matter could have taken for a time that precious form, ought to make matter sacred ever after.

Given this, how might you enhance your view of people, things, and events as sacred and then act out of such a respectful attitude? It's not easy, but it is what everyone is called to do. Doing it can dramatically change your life.

DAY 12
Anger, Gossip, and Reflection

In response to hearing some very negative and vindictive things that some people had said about him, Bishop Maximos said,

> There will always be people who will try to commit some injustice against us. Does this mean that we should be permanently angry? Does it mean

that we must never find peace within ourselves, but always blame others for our anger?

Prayerfulness doesn't move you to react immediately to acts against you. Instead, it encourages you to move from either action (by others) or reaction (by you) to reflection. It is in reflection that you allow God to teach you. When you do learn these lessons, the rewards will be great: peace, a healthy perspective, joy, passion, and true "natural compassion" (rather than the care for others that is induced by duty or guilt).

When you feel yourself ready to speak or behave today in reaction or even retaliation against something done or said to you, move to reflection instead. Such a prayerful process will purify you and allow the rewards of such a purification to then take root in you in possibly new ways.

DAY 13
Let Go . . . Go Deeper

In his book *Christian Zen* William Johnston writes:

How often people get attached to the joyful euphoria of their own [spiritual experience] and they cling to it, they rest in it. And this, I believe, is a form of quietism that hinders progress. John of the Cross speaks of such attachments as the tiny thread around the foot of the bird, hindering it from soaring into the blue sky in serene freedom.

Even though you may feel you have no great experiences in prayer that you need to let go of, you may be holding on to many other experiences, rather than simply enjoying them and moving on in the pilgrimage of life.

How you enjoy what God gives you is important. Once a young novice was looking at a beautiful bowl. His spiritual guide walked by him and said, "Stop committing adultery." The novice recognized that he wasn't speaking about a loss of chastity but about viewing this bowl not with simple admiration but instead with a sense of envy and desire to possess it in a way that leads to a loss of personal freedom.

Today, enjoy whatever interactions, events, and beautiful experiences come your way. But remember not to hold on to them lest they become "spiritually stale." To do so would cause you to miss what other wonderful experiences are coming your way.

DAY 14
Rejecting a Secular Framework

Prayerfulness has us open the door to a new way of seeing and living. Actress Liv Ullman once shared the following deeply felt sentiment:

> I am learning that if I just go on accepting the framework for life that others have given me, if I fail to make my own choices, the reasons for my life will be missing. I will be unable to recognize that which

I have the power to change. I refuse to spend my life regretting the things I failed to do.

See what small things you can do today that may seem silly in the eyes of the world but intuitively you know you would like to do. Maybe it is to:

- smile at a colleague who never greets you;
- write a few lines of freestyle poetry;
- visit a little town you have always wanted to see;
- pray at a time you normally don't;
- study something "totally useless"; or
- lie down on your back and look up at the clouds.

The list can be endless. What would you add to it that you would like to do today?

DAY 15
Being Spiritually Open

Here are two African proverbs that can be helpful as you continue the spiritual journey:

If you refuse to be made straight when you are green, you will not be made straight when you are dry.

Not to know is bad; not to wish to know is worse.

If our prayerfulness is true, then our spiritual mindfulness will be open to the one constant reality in the spiritual life and in all of life in general: *change.*

Practice being intrigued by your feelings, thoughts, and beliefs—especially when they are negative. In your prayer and during your daily musings, allow feelings and thoughts to go through you like a passing train: don't stop them and don't get on board; just notice them as if they were someone else's thoughts or feelings. To face your inner world in this way can result in a newfound self-awareness that is not marked by blame or egoism. And, besides, isn't it fun to learn in such a positive way . . . especially when the learning is about *you?*

DAY 16
Detachment and Compassionate Work

Mother Teresa of Calcutta once said,

> However beautiful the work is, be detached from it, even ready to give it up. The work is not yours. The talents God has given you are not yours; they have been given to you for your use, for the glory of God.

When you are prayerfully detached from your work, you can be more discerning about which crosses God wants you to carry and which ones are of your own choosing. Time devoted to prayer will help you remain grateful and focused on your call. Prayerfulness lets you step back from the many demands of life and ask what God wants of you in a particular situation. Too often, there is a temptation to respond to situations based on the needs of others, the threats of a harsh conscience, or fear of what people might think or how they might react. Such a lack of discernment about difficult choices can have poor consequences—not just for you but for others as well. Business leader John Maxwell describes this quite well in the following story:

> A lighthouse keeper who worked on a rocky stretch of coastline received his new supply of oil once a month to keep the light burning. Not being far from shore, he had frequent guests. One night a woman from the village begged some oil to keep her family warm. Another time a father asked for some to use in his lamp. Another needed some to lubricate a wheel. Since all the requests seemed legitimate, the lighthouse keeper tried to please everyone by granting their requests. Toward the end of the month he noticed the supply of oil was very low. Soon it was gone, and the beacon went out. That night several ships were wrecked and lives were lost. When the authorities investigated, the man was very repentant. To his excuses and pleading their reply was: "You were given oil for one purpose—to keep that light burning!"

What is the one thing God is asking of you in your situation?

DAY 17
Contemplatively Stepping Back

Henri Nouwen reported in *The Genesee Diary* that Abbot John Eudes Bamberger once suggested the following in a spiritual direction session.

> Meditate and explore the small daily events in which you can see your insecurity at work. By meditation you can create distance, and what you can keep at a distance, you can shake off.

With this suggestion in mind, reread the spiritual suggestions on ways to deepen your meditation provided after the chapter entitled "Face Sadness Directly." Let yourself be "spiritually steeped" in these suggestions before you sit and meditate today.

DAY 18
Relations in Life . . . Relations in Prayer

Here's a challenging question that Henri Nouwen once asked himself: "Is it a fact that even in my meditation I relate to the Lord as I relate to people—that is—by manipulation and projection?" In your interactions with others today, including your time with God in meditation, consciously seek to practice not wanting anything from the other—not a smile, agreement, help, information, gratitude . . . *nothing*. This kind of offer of empty space to another is so rare. But it is a worthy practice. Just being present in that way can be an enlightening and spiritually awakening experience for you and a gift for those you meet.

DAY 19
Rest for a Tired Soul

Writer Franz Kafka wrote in his 1911 diary, "Now in the evening, after studying since six o'clock this morning, I noticed how my left hand clasped the fingers of my right hand for a few moments, in sympathy."

Today, take out a few moments to breathe, relax, lean back, and let God nurture you in the moment. One of the greatest gifts you can share with others is a sense of your own peace, but you can't share what you don't have.

Also, one of the greatest ways you can thank God for the amazing gift of your own birth is to take a few moments to enjoy this gift as a child would enjoy a new present at Christmas.

DAY 20
The Precious Gift of Prayerfulness

In a couple of lines from his *Book of Hours* Rilke says to God, "I don't want to think of a place for you. Speak to me from everywhere."

Instead of looking for God in a particular or certain way in meditation or in your daily encounters, recall that true ordinariness is tangible holiness. This will break the chain that confines God to the limits of your preconceived imaginings. You will then be open to seeing God's presence and hearing God's voice in many different and new ways. As we can see in the following reflection given to me by a young adult from Latin America, as well as in our own experience, the awesome beauty of nature reveals God, *if* only we have the eyes to see.

> My spiritual awareness was initially awakened through the stories of my father. My father is a storyteller who, as far as I can remember, always gave meaning to the world through stories. Throughout my early years his metaphors shaped my experiences. Among his wonderfully entertaining stories of fairies and of Greek and Roman mythology (which were particularly meaningful during our time in Greece and Italy), there were countless stories about Mary.
>
> Having been raised in the Latin American tradition, my father had been taught by my grandmother to always pay special reverence to the Virgin Mary. As a result, there are many stories that he regaled to my brother and me while we were growing up. Among them, one of my favorites was the one that my father would often tell as night fell on our house. He would say that the reason it got dark at night was because Mary had laid her cloak over our house to protect us as we slept. These images of Mary, as protector, and Jesus, as comforter and friend, are

images that have stayed with me as I grew up and have shaped my view of religion.

As much as these images made an impression upon me as a child, though, there have been many moments as an adult that I have also deeply sensed the presence of God in my life in amazing ways. Many of these have been moments of experiencing nature in an intense way when I have felt, quite tangibly, God's love for me. One of these memories is particularly fresh in my mind until this day and involves the light of the moon. It had taken place a number of years ago when I was a teenager and visiting relatives in Costa Rica.

We had gone to stay with my uncle and his in-laws for the weekend. They owned a small ranch, hours from the busy and congested capital city, out toward the Pacific Ocean. I remember pulling up to the ranch after several hours of driving on the back roads that were meant only for traveling on horseback. It was incredibly remote, with no other humans in the surrounding areas for miles.

That night after dinner, my family went for a stroll. We needed a flashlight to shine our way as we walked. The crickets chirped, the breeze rustled the leaves, and the only sounds in the still night were the small rocks crunching under our feet. To demonstrate to us the intensity of the darkness that enveloped us, my father turned off the flashlight for what felt like several minutes, but which probably lasted only seconds. I had never experienced such darkness. I could not even see my hand in front of my face. It was amazing and scary at the same time.

When we turned, headed back, and finally came upon the house, my uncle's father-in-law was standing by the door to greet us. I ran up to him, excited to tell our story about the adventure in the dark. He explained that the moon hadn't come up yet, but that if I were patient, he would show me something else that was even more incredible than the darkness I had experienced.

We then walked out to the fence that surrounded the ranch and waited. I was not sure how much time had passed but suddenly he pointed ahead and asked me to watch. Ever so slowly light began to break behind what eventually revealed itself as a mountain. Behind it the moon slowly started to rise. As it did, the stars that had been glowing so brightly just moments before immediately receded. Below the pasture began to light up as well, and I was finally able to make out the shapes of trees and bushes where before everything had been black. It was as though the scenery that had previously been hidden was slowly being uncovered in front of my very eyes. I was in a state of complete awe. What had previously been pitch dark was now beautifully lit up by the near full moon—a breathtaking portrait of God's creation for all to see.

We have these memories and experiences in our past, too. They are examples of "God speaking to us from everywhere." For a moment or two, reflect back on such experiences in your own life. Then, after doing that, consider how you might position yourself to be open to experience such possibilities of awe in the future. Secular eyes see so little. Prayerful eyes can embrace so much. We do have a choice. How we choose can determine what our life is like and the spirit in which it is lived.

DAY 21
Flowing with God

Robert Ellsberg in his fine work *The Saints' Guide to Happiness* writes,

> So often we measure our identity and success by how well we remain in control. But in the end the final meaning of our lives may be determined as much by our capacity to trust, to let go, to place ourselves in the hands of another.

The following story by a young priest and counselor from the Pacific island kingdom of Tonga illustrates how, when we do this, we can meet the surprising gift of God's mercy.

> I still remember a particular incident several years ago when after a game of rugby I went with some friends to enjoy a few drinks. After the drinking

session, my friends and I stole two piglets from home. I was scared that my father would punish me—not because of the pigs, but because of stealing and not respecting our property.

My friends and I ate the pigs, but afterward I came home and packed my clothes and books and went to stay at one of my friend's houses. Throughout that week I felt empty, incomplete, lonely, lost, and could not concentrate on my studies. Deep inside my heart I felt that the sun had already set on me. To make matters worse I did not turn up for rugby training and instead isolated myself from my teammates for a week. I really wanted to return home, but was scared of the consequences I would face.

The following weekend I did decide to go back home and seek my dad's forgiveness. I felt like the prodigal son in the Gospel of Luke who, after having wasted his share of his wealth and hitting rock bottom, came to his senses, realizing that only his father would save him. Only his father could give his life and the hope to live back to him again.

When I opened the door, I saw my dad quietly sitting there, saying nothing. In his gospel account, Luke states that when the father saw his son coming he had compassion, stood up, ran, embraced, and kissed him. When I walked into the house and my dad saw me, he did not run to me but instead looked down and started to cry.

My father's reaction caught me totally by surprise, as I was expecting to be yelled at and maybe even chased out from our home. I likened my father's tears to the holy water used in baptism, to bring the newly baptized child into new life, making the new child a son of God and a sanctuary of the Holy Spirit.

I never really understood the depth of my father's love for me until that moment on that day. I used to question whether my dad loved me or not. However, on that very morning I was convinced that he loved me more than I expected, and it took me messing up big time to truly fathom it.

I walked straight up to my dad, kissed, and sat beside him for a while. We did not exchange any words but both cried for quite a while. I then apologized for what I did, and my father forgave me. He then quoted the words of Jesus in the gospel that no father would give his son a stone if he asked for bread or a snake if he asked for a fish. As I think back to what my father said, I know he was trying to tell me, "Son, I love and forgive you."

I remember that day as one of the happiest of my life. I felt that the sun rose again on my life. I was as excited as someone just released from custody or prison. I felt light like an eagle spreading its wings to embrace the winds floating peacefully in the air. I now felt extremely energized and wanted to live as a person of compassion who forgives no matter what

has been done to me. In a phrase, I felt reborn and
renewed again.

Are there events in your life that have freed you in this
way? Do you remember them when you are called to be
compassionate? Can you see all of this as ways God is calling you to flow with God by trusting those in your life who
love you? These are all important questions to ponder as
you journey prayerfully through today and the rest of your
life.

DAY 22
Letting Criticism Free You Up

Once when I received sharp critical feedback, I was
graced with the experience of God's love and the following
accompanying insight: *everything said about you, no matter
how poor the motivation of the person saying it, is true to some
extent.* So, if such information can be mined, it can teach
us and free us in ways that success and positive feedback
could never do.

Think about experiences you have had when you
received stinging criticism from someone you believe neither likes nor values your achievements. Despite this person's feelings and/or your own, what lessons *about yourself*
can be learned from what this person has said or done? (If
it is a recent occurrence, you may need to wait a bit before
you are ready to do this.)

DAY 23
Guidelines for Spiritual Freedom

Each of us is "unfree" in many ways. When you are spiritually mindful, you seek to uncover and understand your resistance to change and growth. Use one or all of these guidelines to reflect on spiritual freedom:

- Being in the now and meeting both the peaceful and the painful as well as the familiar and unfamiliar leads to an acceptance of all realities and following what is good.
- Facing your fears, doubts, boredom, anxieties, anger, charlatanism, and manipulative nature doesn't require much courage when you have humility.
- A confining or static image of God may prevent you from having the inner freedom that comes with true prayerfulness. This inner freedom leads to an opportunity to experience God in so many dynamic new ways.

Reflecting slowly on any of the above lessons in spiritual mindfulness that strike you as particularly helpful at this particular time in your life can further soften your soul. A softened soul welcomes freedom and allows you to see and absorb the changes that are necessary for you at this time.

DAY 24
"This Too, This Too . . ."

Jack Kornfield, in his Eastern spirituality work *A Path with Heart*, notes:

> I had hoped for special effects from meditation—happiness, special states of rapture, extraordinary experiences. But that was not primarily what my teacher offered. He offered a way of life, a lifelong path of awakening, attention, surrender, and commitment. He offered a happiness that was not dependent on any of the changing conditions of the world but came out of one's own difficult and conscious inner transformation. In joining the monastery, I had hoped to leave behind the pain of my family life and the difficulties of the world, but of course they followed me. It took many years for me to realize that these difficulties were part of my practice. . . . The simple phrase, "This too, this too," was the main meditation instruction of [another of the spiritual masters] with whom I studied. Through these few words we were encouraged to soften and open to see whatever we encountered, accepting the truth with a wise and understanding heart.

Including all of the specifics of your life is what makes your prayerfulness rich. When something joyful, puzzling, sad, or upsetting happens—no matter how little it seems at first—remember to say in prayer, "This too, this too."

Seeing even distractions as sources for new knowledge will reap great rewards. The goal of this approach is to transform all of your life into your spiritual life. In this way, rather than being tied down by so many other "voices" (culture, peer pressure, family fears, or neediness) in your life, you can respond to God's sometimes soft voice that is calling you to new freedom and living more fully.

Try to incorporate "this too, this too" into your own spiritual awareness today to see how it can enhance your sense of prayerfulness.

DAY 25
Acceptance of Yourself

After a morning meditation period, a spiritual guide said to those present, "Each of you is perfect the way you are." Then, after a short pause, he added with a smile, "And, you can all use a little improvement."

When you truly accept yourself, you can have the courage to acknowledge the many gifts God has given you. And in the same vein, you honestly face your own growing edges. This allows you to avoid the perils of extreme self-confidence on the one hand or extreme self-doubt on the other.

And, when you accept yourself with a spirit of intrigue, you can see how your gifts (such as, perhaps, faithfulness or enthusiasm) can turn into unwanted or defensive behavior (such as, perhaps, rigidity or exhibitionism) under some circumstances.

DAY 26
Perseverance in Prayer

An accomplished publisher of poetry met with his spiritual teacher. He told him that he had been meditating for over a year and a half and that he just couldn't continue at this point because every time he sat down to meditate, he started to cry. He said, "I can't take it anymore." And said he was leaving.

The spiritual master didn't say he should stay but merely added, "You try and you try and you fail, and then you go deeper."

When have you been tempted to abandon your regular time in prayer, your commitment to seeing where God's hand may be in unappealing or unwanted situations, or your continued works of compassion? What did you learn from these situations?

DAY 27
Good Words

In the fourth century, one desert father complained, "We used to get together and build each other up in the Spirit. Now all we do is gossip." How often and unfortunately natural it is to speak about others in a negative way. Sometimes you don't even know you are doing it or how to stop. The Dalai Lama had what I think is a unique approach, though. He said, "If you find yourself slandering anybody, first imagine that your mouth is filled with excrement. It will break you of the habit quickly enough."

Today, be especially vigilant about any negative comments you are inclined to make about people behind their backs. Even if what you say is true, what does it accomplish? Before you say something, recall that it will (or should) make you feel some regret later—even if you partially fool yourself into believing that you meant well.

DAY 28
Role Models

Sandy Johnson wrote, in her enjoyable work *The Book of Tibetan Elders*, that she received the following advice: "When you see a person who is, as you say, enlightened, and you wish you would be able to attain their qualities, it is very important that you put this wish into action."

Think of people in your life with personalities similar to your own or with whom you can readily identify for some other reason. Within that group identify those who you feel are more centered, open, gentle, clear, passionate, and focused than you are. Now, ask yourself what the ways are of thinking and behaving demonstrated by them that you can imitate—especially in how they handle negative experiences and appreciate life.

DAY 29
Living Kindness

Mother Teresa of Calcutta was fond of saying, "Kindness has converted more people than zeal, science, or eloquence."

In what ways are you kind?

What would kindness look like in you with a bit more effort?

How can your acts of kindness be offered not as a sacrifice, duty, or mere exercise but instead from a deep appreciation of how you are truly blessed?

DAY 30
The Courage to Live

Richard Bode in his wonderful book *First You Have to Row a Little Boat* writes:

> The day will come when I will die. So the only matter of consequence before me is what I will do with my allotted time. I can remain on shore, paralyzed with fear, or I can raise my sails and dip and soar in the breeze.

This whole thirty-day personal retreat on navigating your spiritual life has been about St. Iraeneus's comment, "The glory of God is a human being fully alive, for our true life is the vision of God."

How do you plan to raise your "spiritual and psychological sails" and prayerfully dip and soar in the breeze of life over the next month? Feel free to list specifics for yourself in response to this question so you can then, in turn, be inspired to act in specific ways to change your life. (General goals usually don't amount to much.)

Extending Your Retreat

Now that you have completed this retreat you may find it helpful to return to a particular day that was meaningful for you. You may also want to continue a process of daily reflection on prayerfulness. You can do this by selecting one of the guidelines for prayerful living to reflect on each day.

- Real compassion, rather than a caring that is based on guilt or duty, connects you with others in a way that fosters integration within yourself as well.
- Spiritual disciplines should include offering a gentle space to others; finding quiet, honest space within yourself; and receiving guidance from others so both spaces remain pure of grasping and the desire for gain.
- Meditation is made up of a little technique and a lot of gentle love.
- Sadness may come in the silence because that is when this hidden teacher may feel welcome to show her helpful face as a reminder that you may

be holding onto something less than the Truth (God).

- Once you let the pain of an interpersonal encounter wash over and away from you, what is left is a clean truth about yourself that a more relaxed encounter could not produce in a million years.
- Acknowledge easily and openly both what you have been praised and condemned for, and where there was once negative passion will be new wisdom and the continued freedom only humility can bring.
- Strong emotions are always the smoke of the fire of attachment.
- See both a beautiful sunny morning and a relaxing rainy afternoon as reminders that love is around you and that the hurt, doubt, and resentment you may have are little parts of your life that need to be released.
- Life is no longer small and unrewarding when you get excited about how you can grow spiritually and be naturally compassionate.
- Flowing with life doesn't stop the pain; nothing can do that. Yet it does lessen unnecessary suffering, teach new lessons, and help one to see the value of having patience for new openings. As Thomas Merton says: "Courage comes and goes; hold on for the next supply."
- Spirituality is not designed to make you special. True ordinariness is tangible holiness.

- Every period in your life brings new gifts. If you use old techniques, your attitudes fail to change; you won't be able to open those gifts.
- Persons who really love inner freedom demonstrate it by being open to seeing specific truths about themselves without resentment, hostility, or fear.
- Being able to enjoy life as it is given takes practice, whereas thinking wistfully about life is easy.
- Spiritual persons enjoy life's daily wealth, while those around them dream of silly things like wealth, fame, power, and others finding them attractive.
- Those who respect everyone have many spiritual teachers.
- Anthony de Mello used to tell people, "It is easier to put on slippers than to carpet the whole of the earth." Perspective that comes with being prayerful prevents you from entering "the carpeting business."
- Embarrassment, failure, and awkwardness are the salvific handles of God's grace.
- What people call "happiness" is often really a passing high, after which they will have a corresponding low.
- One of the greatest gifts you can give yourself is to observe yourself with interest but not judgment.
- Being prayerful, open, and free often requires that you forgo pleasing family members (both living and dead) and friends.
- Take from every positive role model something to practice in life.

- While you need to be open to all people, you must develop and nurture a circle of friends who will challenge, support, nurture, and inspire you (as well as make you laugh when you need to!).
- If you wish to be free in spirit only for yourself, then you have failed already; if you wish to be free for others too, your compassionate purpose will purify you.

A Spiritual Mindfulness
Questionnaire (SMQ)

Discovering Your Own
Prayerfulness Profile

A s we have seen, prayerfulness is being in the now with a sense of openness to experiencing God in the world and yourself in dynamic new ways. The Spiritual Mindfulness Questionnaire (SMQ) is designed to help you gain a clearer sense of how open, present, and prayerful you are in your daily life. After you complete this questionnaire, as you review your responses with the support of the reflection guide provided, you will have information as to where you can most profitably direct your attention to improve your own sense of prayerfulness and awareness at this point in your journey.

The SMQ should also give you a better indication of what is pulling you into the past or preoccupying you with the future rather than allowing you to be in the present, the place where the living God wants to be with you. The information you can glean from your responses to this questionnaire should also help you to discover such important information as what your regular prayer practices are; what your approach to meditation is; how supportive your community of friends is; how to better flow with your life rather than drift or run away from it; whether you are naturally compassionate instead of caring for others merely out of duty or guilt; and what is robbing you of, or can enhance, your joy and peace.

The SMQ was created to complement the classic and contemporary literature on discernment, contemplation, and spiritual mindfulness. It covers a good deal of ground and should produce a wide range of information for self-reflection, discernment with your spiritual director, or discussions with a close friend with whom you wish to share your journey.

Before beginning to respond to the SMQ, take out a few moments of quiet time to center yourself. Then, on a separate sheet of paper, after reading each question, write the first thing that comes to your mind as a response. Don't labor over your responses. There are no right or wrong answers—just your answers. You are the primary expert on your own spiritual life and experiences.

Be as clear and transparent as you can, and don't go back to previous questions once you have finished with them. Remember you can always visit this questionnaire again in the future. For now, you want to get your initial sense of how you are living in the Spirit and what produces either joy and peace or difficulty and anxiety for you.

The themes that arise from this questionnaire will enable you to create a prayerfulness profile of yourself. You will uncover wonderfully helpful information that will highlight what is encouraging you to be or discouraging you from being in the now, seeking a sense of God's presence in all things. It will enable you to have an openness to hear the good news that all things—including you—are being made new each day.

The process is simple, the information quite helpful. The only ground rule is to answer honestly and clearly. The more transparent you are, the more useful the information will be to you.

Now, please take a few moments of silence before you begin.

Spiritual Mindfulness Questionnaire

1. In your own life, how do you approach the people you meet and the ordinary activities of each day so that they become sacred?
2. What preoccupies you in ways that seem to prevent you from seeing God?
3. Are you someone who listens to others, or do you find that much of the time you are simply hearing them out while waiting for your opportunity to speak?
4. What unfinished business from the past seems to continually intrude upon your present peace, and how do you address it in a prayerful way?

5. When and how do you regularly meditate?
6. Do you feel deprived of happiness because there are certain elements or people missing in your life?
7. What experiences—regardless of their outcomes—provide you with the greatest satisfaction?
8. Who in your circle of friends encourages a life of spiritual awareness, prayer, meaning, and compassion?
9. Who and what are the most annoying people and situations for you, and what can they teach you?
10. What do you believe robs you of your joy and peace?
11. How much of the day would you say you "live in the now"?
12. When you are not in the present, what approaches do you use to return yourself to the now?
13. What thoughts or past behaviors make you feel so vulnerable, ashamed, or anxious that you want to deny, avoid, run away, or get angry when they come to mind?
14. Who are your role models, and how do you seek to emulate them?
15. What do you believe is the secret of happiness?
16. What are you living for, and what—at times—do you believe prevents you from living that way?
17. When do you feel most alive and least focused on yourself? When do you experience that you are flowing with your life rather than drifting through it?
18. Under what conditions are you most apt to be "mindless" rather than mindful? How do you address this when you realize it?

19. When you think of moments in the past when you felt most present, mindful, and grateful to God, what do these experiences teach you about living mindfully now?

20. Do you value patience enough to try to observe yourself when you start to hurry life along? What helps you stop, lean back into the now, and change your pace and way of facing things?

21. What are the factors that contribute to your grasping at what you want or hanging on to what you like, and why is it problematic for you to let go?

22. In prayer and life are you able to let your thoughts arise without judging, cutting off, entertaining, or trying to suppress them? Can you see them like a cloud passing overhead and simply take note of and merely allow them to pass on?

23. Are there parts of your day when striving, surviving, and accomplishing are not necessary, and just "being" and "allowing" are your mindset?

24. Do you find yourself rejecting or resigning yourself to situations, or are you able to observe without judgment and accept situations so you can truly learn what they have to teach you?

25. Do you fully relish what is put before you in life, or do you make comparisons?

26. How much do you think habit figures into your daily life? What can you do about this?

27. What part does being spiritually mindful have to do with your relationships?

28. What practical ways do you use to encourage yourself to be spiritually mindful at home, work, church, and during leisure activities?

29. How do you determine whether a desire to do something is a call from God or is borne of inordinate self-interest, self-doubt, peer pressure, or cultural values?

30. In what ways are you spiritually and psychologically seeking to be open and receptive to God's voice, in the familiar and unfamiliar, and in your interior and exterior experiences during the day?

Suggestions for Navigating Your Responses to the SMQ

Below are comments on each question. Hopefully, they will spur on your conversation with yourself and help you reflect on your responses. If they are helpful, wonderful. If some of them are not, then simply move on to the next question.

1. In your own life, how do you approach the people you meet and the ordinary activities of each day so that they become sacred?

When people speak about "the *spiritual* life," it is often because they feel something in their daily life is lacking. There is still a divide between the heart of their life where they meet God and the rest of their activities and interactions during the day. This question is designed to raise awareness of the need to make *all* of life spiritual through new approaches to spiritual mindfulness. This may require a shift in the way you are thinking about prayerfulness now. When you can see all of life as spiritual, you can begin to live as fully as God would have you do. (Once again, living fully is to love God deeply, do what you can for others, and take care of yourself as an act of gratitude for the life you have been given.)

2. What preoccupies you in ways that seem to prevent you from seeing God?

A life with inner freedom begins where your demands, needs, and self-interest end. Spiritual clarity takes place during those times when you are a person without guile, transparent, open to seeing the unfamiliar and possibly unlikable because you wish to see the truth and learn from it. To do that you need to have trust that no matter what you learn—even if you don't like it—all will be well.

3. Are you someone who listens to others, or do you find that much of the time you are simply hearing them out while waiting for your opportunity to speak?

Listening is a spiritually mindful activity, whereas merely half-listening or hearing while you are patiently waiting for your opportunity to speak is not. This question is a prompt to be more attentive to those around you. This is not only an act of respect for them but also for God, who is continually speaking to you through our environment and our inner reactions to it. Remember, discernment of God's will comes through others and what others say to you. You see this when you move beyond your own reactions to reflection. But you can't do that if you are not in tune with what others are saying to you and if you are reacting, rather than fully listening.

4. **What unfinished business from the past seems to continually intrude upon your present peace, and how do you address it in a prayerful way?**

Prayerfulness requires you to be in the now with God. Too often you may be caught in the silver casket of nostalgia or preoccupied with something in the past. Allowing the past to come through you like a slowly moving train without your preventing it or stopping it can teach you and allow you to remain in the present. Knowing as much of your unfinished business as possible can help to avoid being drawn into it when you are quiet.

5. **When and how do you regularly meditate?**

This basic question is designed to help you become more aware that for meditation and contemplation to be powerful, it must be done regularly—even if it is only for a few minutes. It must become part of your life until you realize that your life and activities come out of it. Thomas Merton had only a few hours each day to write in the monastery. Yet, at one point, he kept two secretaries busy transcribing his work. How did he do this? Dom Eudes Bamberger believed it was because his writings were fruits of his prayer life.

6. **Do you feel deprived of happiness because there are certain elements or people missing in your life?**

Life is like a passing train. Do you wait for just the right person or event to arrive before you start living? Or, are you living each moment as a gift from God?

7. What experiences—regardless of their outcomes—provide you with the greatest satisfaction?

Having preferences is natural. However, there is a fine line between having preferences and preferences having you. On a very basic level, you may like to eat dinner at a particular time, and that's all well and good. But, if that time is changed for some reason and you react to it strongly, then it isn't fine. You have lost your freedom. When you add up such little losses of freedom, they can be like invisible puppeteers pulling you in directions that destroy your peace and negatively affect others as well.

8. Who in your circle of friends encourages a life of spiritual awareness, prayer, meaning, and compassion?

The type of friends you have is crucial to your spiritual life—even if they are persons you see only once in a while but stay in touch with via e-mail or by phone. The classic four voices that I think need to be present first include the prophet who asks the question: what voices are guiding you in life? The second is the cheerleader who is sympathetic and supportive. The third is the teaser or harasser who helps you not take yourself too seriously as you sincerely seek to take God's call to heart. The final is the spiritual friend who calls you to be all that you can be without embarrassing you about where you are at this point. (More can be read about these types of friends in either of the books *Touching the Holy* or *Bounce*.)

9. Who and what are the most annoying people and situations for you, and what can they teach you?

Annoying people are often ignored, avoided, or criticized. That's natural, of course. Rarely are they seen as a special source of wisdom—even as a "teacher" of a sort, and therefore, the lessons they can teach are missed. You can learn a lot about yourself when you ask, "What about this person is especially annoying to *me*?" Other people would not even be bothered by them, but you are at some point to some degree. Why? If you take this little question seriously, it is possible to gain much heretofore unfathomed knowledge about yourself. This can not only add to self-knowledge but can also change for the better how you interact with others.

10. What do you believe robs you of your joy and peace?

This question is in line with the one above. In reality, no one should be able to rob you of your joy and peace; it is given to you by God. Why—in twelve-step language—you allow some people or situations to "rent space in your head" is your problem. By understanding this problem you can truly become free of the psychological and spiritual chains you may have put on yourself. So, the question again, with slightly different phrasing is: what power are you giving away, and why are you doing so, to persons who key off something in you that results in your loss of peace and joy?

11. How much of the day would you say you "live in the now"?

Recognizing how often you are caught in a web of thought about the past or future is somewhat discouraging. But it can also be quite helpful if you view it correctly. When you see how you are not attending to what is in front of you, you can lean back or move forward into the now and be fully alive in the present. When you do this you can still reflect on the past at times but not be trapped by it. You will also be able to plan for the future, not be preoccupied with it. Furthermore, you can recognize that by doing this you will be more and more drawn into the moment in front of you, which holds so much if you let it. Remember James Joyce's comment about a character in one of his books: "Mr. Duffy lived a short distance from his body." How often are you existing in this way rather than living in the now?

12. When you are not in the present, what approaches do you use to return yourself to the now?

Having simple techniques to bring yourself back to the present is important. It may just be taking a few breaths, focusing on the person or task at hand, or saying a centering word for a few seconds. A simple technique can be powerful if you can use it without judging yourself (which may cause discouragement). You need only to recognize that your attention to the moment has wandered and call yourself to back to where you are now.

13. What thoughts or past behaviors make you feel so vulnerable, ashamed, or anxious that you want to

deny, avoid, run away, or get angry when they come to mind?

Knowing the sensitive points in your psyche is essential in order to recognize when they have been irritated and are keeping you from living freely. When there are issues in your life that you haven't faced directly or come to terms with, they can hold sway over you. They drain the energy you could use for creative living rather than for defensiveness.

14. Who are your role models, and how do you seek to emulate them?

Having role models is very important to your spiritual journey. It is especially helpful if they are similar to you but more actualized and spiritually developed. Imitate your role models when you find yourself in difficult situations. Though difficult, such situations can offer you the chance to experience new, healthy perspectives, peace, and joy. They are a chance to practice sound, spiritual ways of living, reflecting, and responding. Unless you seek to actively imitate your role models, you run the risk of simply reacting to difficult situations in unhelpful ways, or only viewing your role models wistfully as wonderful people who are in reality impossible for you to imitate.

15. What do you believe is the secret of happiness?

How you identify "the secret of happiness" will tell you a lot about yourself. Do you see the secret as something outside of yourself or something within you? If there is a "secret to happiness," it is simply to be fully alive, and to know when you are not. And further, to understand that this is not because of your environment, but because of something within you.

16. What are you living for, and what—at times—do you believe prevents you from living that way?

This question posed by Merton encourages each of us to take note of exactly what our philosophy of life is and where the blocks to living that way are. "Where your treasure is, your heart is," Jesus said (Mt 6:21). If this is true, then you need to recognize that the place where you are putting all your energy is what you are actually living for, whether you wish to admit it or not. Your actions and preoccupations tell a lot about you. Identify them and you will have a sense of who or what your "god" is. For instance, what do you think about when you go to bed at night? What fills your mind and heart as you drive or walk? The answers to these and similar questions will tell you what, in fact, you are really living for. Prayerful persons recognize the challenges in their world, family, workplace, and religious denomination or community. They are also able to figure out what is causing these problems and how to deal with them. While most of us try to do something about our problems, it is the prayerful person who, after recognizing the source, planning, and doing, is able to step back and let God take care of the rest. That is something we all need to do if we are to be serious about God's role in our lives as well as our role in the divine plan.

17. **When do you feel most alive and least focused on yourself? When do you experience that you are flowing with your life rather than drifting through it?**

When you flow with life, you are spiritually mindful. You do feel relaxed and happily involved, regardless of the results. Your contemplation and meditation are like that as well. All of life can be like this when you are prayerful and motivated rather than competitive, grasping, and fearful.

18. **Under what conditions are you most apt to be "mind-less" rather than mindful? How do you address this when you realize it?**

There are times when all of us are very mindless, distracted, and inattentive. Knowing that when this occurs it is a call to focus more in those circumstances will in turn lead to more living and less existing or rushing through your day. You don't want to be so driven in life that you miss what is important. Reflect on these questions: In what ways do you come back when you've drifted into mindless behavior? How do you prayerfully call yourself back home?

19. **When you think of moments in the past when you felt most present, mindful, and grateful to God, what do these experiences teach you about living mindfully now?**

This question can encourage you to appreciate how mindful you already are, perhaps without realizing it. Also, knowing about these moments can help you to see how wonderful it is to be present in the now with your eyes wide open to how God is blessing you.

20. **Do you value patience enough to try to observe yourself when you start to hurry life along? What helps you stop, lean back into the now, and change your pace and way of facing things?**

Patience is at the heart of the spiritual life. Many of us get so discouraged when we realize we are not being patient, but that only makes things worse. Instead remember that the moment you find yourself being impatient is an ideal time to slow down, pay attention, and live.

21. **What are the factors that contribute to your grasping at what you want or hanging on to what you like, and why is it problematic for you to let go?**

The best way to let go is not to hold on in the first place! Knowing what, how, and to whom you cling is very valuable information. It will help you see that enjoying something and desiring to possess it are two different things. This question also taps into the insecurities that need to be faced and gently explored, without harsh judgment. A mentor is often very helpful in dealing with responses on the topic of grasping or hanging on, since it is possible to make even the most beautiful things a cause for unnecessary concern when there is a tendency to hold on too tightly.

22. **In prayer and life are you able to let your thoughts arise without judging, cutting off, entertaining, or trying to suppress them? Can you see them like a**

cloud passing overhead and simply take note of and merely allow them to pass on?

Most people have thoughts that are particularly disturbing to them. One way to handle this is to welcome your thoughts gently while holding them at a distance. In other words, act as if they were being experienced by someone else. If you can look at your thoughts honestly and kindly, then the temptation to project the blame on others and be resentful, or to condemn yourself for these thoughts, will be lessened. You will learn more, and this will lead to greater freedom.

23. Are there parts of your day when striving, surviving, and accomplishing are not necessary and just "being" and "allowing" are your mindset?

This question points you to look at the place where the spirit thrives. These are the times when you flow with your day rather than drift through, rush by, or attack it. Being, rather than just doing, is at the heart of being a reflective presence to yourself and others. When you are not that way, a lot of stress and hardship can result.

24. Do you find yourself rejecting or resigning yourself to situations, or are you able to observe without judgment and accept situations so you can truly learn what they have to teach you?

Many people tend to label life. But this can lead you to quickly reject something or resign yourself to it rather than look for what it can teach you. In meditation, for instance, you will at certain points face boredom. As was previously mentioned, spiritual masters often say that if you are bored for two minutes, then do it for four! Facing your life directly and with discipline, you can find so much that you might normally miss by judging and quickly acting. Resist labeling, and seek to fully fathom what you might learn about yourself and God through your daily interactions.

25. Do you fully relish what is put before you in life, or do you make comparisons?

Comparison and a sense of entitlement—"I deserve something and want more"—often keep people from appreciating the depth of the gift before them. People who live with gratitude and spiritual mindfulness form a circle of grace with these two attitudes and find there is always so much to appreciate in their lives.

26. How much do you think habit figures into your daily life? What can you do about this?

Habit is the enemy of the spiritually aware life. The more aware you are, the more you can keep habit to a minimum so that you are alive more of the time.

27. What part does being spiritually mindful have to do with your relationships?

Relationships deepen when you are attentive to another rather than lost in your head or letting your mind wander. When you eat, eat. When you are riding a bike, ride. When you are in a relationship, be there. Know how to encourage a sense of presence in yourself.

28. **What practical ways do you use to encourage yourself to be spiritually mindful at home, work, church, and during leisure activities?**

This question examines your approach to spiritual mindfulness or prayerfulness during your daily routine. This is helpful because it raises sensitivity to the wonderful techniques and attitudes you already know and have in place that can make you more prayerful and alive.

29. **How do you determine whether a desire to do something is a call from God or is borne of inordinate self-interest, self-doubt, peer pressure, or cultural values?**

The fruits of discernment are a sense of freedom and peace. These help you to know whether the desire you have is a call from God or from another, far lesser voice (success, peer pressure, competition, power, control, financial gain, etc.). These lesser calls can be fine in and of themselves, and responding to them is part of being alive. The real question, though, is whether in a particular instance such calls are drowning out the voice of God. Contemplative Thomas Merton once asked whether people do what they want and then ask God to bless it, or if they first ask God what is wanted of them and then seek to do it. When our will and God's will intersect, freedom and love are the result.

30. **In what ways are you spiritually and psychologically seeking to be open and receptive to God's voice, in the familiar and unfamiliar, and in your interior and exterior experiences during the day?**

Being open to the unfamiliar and the familiar, the unattractive as well as the attractive, is part of being a discerning person. You must be willing to be uncomfortable and challenged. This is not something people normally wish for themselves. Yet, by meditating and reflecting during the day with a spirit of intrigue, you will often be able with the grace of God to forgo the dangers of arrogance (projecting the blame on others), ignorance (self-condemnation), or discouragement (possibly because you want instant results). Intrigue about your inner life and what is happening in your life can flourish when you have a balance between kindness and clarity in how you perceive everything you are experiencing and feeling, in what you are thinking, and in the ways you are behaving. When you have too much kindness, you will probably have little or no growth. On the other hand, when you have clarity without kindness, you can hurt yourself. This is what some psychologists refer to as "causing narcissistic injury."

I hope the above comments and questions were of help in exploring your own responses. There is so much fascinating and potentially helpful information in the way you answered. Please continue to examine your responses again and again as you move through the pilgrimage we call "the spiritual life." By doing that, prayerfulness or spiritual mindfulness will continually be seen in new, much richer ways, and you will be able to meet the goal of all prayerfulness that God sets before us: *to live more fully.*

Epilogue

Living Fully: The Goal of Prayerfulness

P rayerfulness, in the end, is about the most basic wish God has for us: *to live fully*. This occurs when God's will (theonomy) and our will (autonomy) are one. When we live that way, our compassion is rich and natural; our prayer is deep rather than flat; and our self-care, self-knowledge, and self-love are fired by gratitude to God for the precious gift of life. However, we know this is easier said than done unless we possess a simplicity of faith, which is at the heart of the spiritual life and helps us see clearly even when times are tough.

A friend of mine who is a Jesuit priest and scripture scholar was at his mother's bedside in the final days of her life. At one point, he asked her, "Mom, are you afraid about what happens next?" To which she replied quite calmly, "No, John. I'm not afraid. Just very curious." That's faith. That's simplicity. That's a trust in God we all should pray to have.

Prayerfulness both feeds and is an outgrowth of faith—faith like my friend's mother had. It helps us live fully and die well when the time comes. And that is what this book has been all about. And so, by way of closing, I offer you the following wish written by an unknown Celtic author:

An Irish Blessing

> I wish you not a path devoid of clouds,
> Nor a life on a bed of roses,
> Nor that you might never need regret,
> Nor that you should never feel pain.
>
> No, that is not my wish for you.
>
> My wish for you is:
>
> That you might be brave in times of trial,
> When others lay crosses upon your shoulders.
> When mountains must be climbed and chasms are to be crossed;
> When hope scarce can shine through.
>
> That every gift God gave you might grow along with you
> And let you give the gift of joy to all who care for you.
> That you may always have a friend who is worth that name,
> Whom you can trust, and who helps you in times of sadness,
> Who will defy the storms of daily life at your side.

One more wish I have for you:
That in every hour of joy and pain
You may feel God close to you.

This is my wish for you, and all who care for you.

This is my hope for you, now and forever.

Recommended Readings on Prayer, Prayerfulness, and Spiritual Mindfulness

There are many wonderful books on meditation, prayerfulness, and spiritual mindfulness/awareness. I am sure you have your own favorites, but I wanted to mention several of mine that may be of support to you in your spiritual life. The ones that I read and reread again come from certain authors, some who are well-known and others who may not be. Those below that you have read before but haven't reviewed recently might be worth another look. If they are worthy books, they will have grown with you and may be of use in ways that were impossible in the past. I hope you find a few new favorites in the list as well.

Anonymous. *The Cloud of Unknowing*
Anthony Bloom. *Beginning to Pray*
Jerry Braza. *Moment by Moment*
Phil Cousineau. *The Art of Pilgrimage*
Dalai Lama. *The Path to Tranquility*
Paula D'Arcy. *A New Set of Eyes*
Anthony de Mello. *Sadhana*

————. *One Minute Wisdom*

Esther de Waal. *Lost in Wonder*

Christina Feldman. *Compassion*

Peter France. *Hermits*

Mary Margaret Funk. *Thoughts Matter*

Ivone Gebara. *Mary, Mother of God, Mother of the Poor*

Bhante Henepola Gunaratana. *Mindfulness in Plain English*

Thich Nhat Hanh. *The Miracle of Mindfulness*

Abraham Heschel. *I Asked for Wonder*

Elizabeth Johnson. *Quest for the Living God*

Jon Kabat-Zinn. *Wherever You Go, There You Are*

Thomas Keating. *Reawakenings*

Jack Kornfield *A Path with Heart*

————. *After the Ecstasy, the Laundry*

Brother Lawrence of the Resurrection. *In the Presence of God*

Kathleen Norris. *Dakota*

Henri Nouwen. *Making All Things New*

————. *Way of the Heart*

————. *Return of the Prodigal Son*

————. *The Genesee Diary*

Thomas Merton. *New Seeds of Contemplation*

————. *A Thomas Merton Reader*

————. *Contemplative Prayer*

————. *Spiritual Direction and Meditation*

Basil Pennington. *Centering Prayer*

Joyce Rupp. *Prayer*

David Steindl-Rast. *Gratefulness*

Sharon Salzberg. *Insight Meditation*

Anthony Storr. *Solitude*
Shunryu Suzuki. *Not Always So*
Evelyn Underhill. *The Spiritual Life*
Andrew Weiss. *Beginning Mindfulness*
Robert Wicks. *Everyday Simplicity*
Paramahansa Yogananda. *In the Sanctuary of the Soul*

Sources

Albom, Mitch. *Tuesdays with Morrie*. New York: Doubleday, 1997.

Bloom, Anthony. *Beginning to Pray*. Mahwah, NJ: Paulist Press, 1970.

Bode, Richard. *First You Have to Row a Little Boat*. New York: Warner, 1993.

Braza, Jerry. *Moment by Moment*. New York: Tuttle, 1997.

Brazier, David. *Zen Therapy*. New York: Wiley, 1995.

Brod, Max. *Kafka*. New York: Da Capo, 1995.

Chadwick, David. *The Crooked Cucumber*. New York: Broadway, 1999.

Chodron, Pema. *When Things Fall Apart*. Boston: Shambhala, 1997.

Ciarrocchi, Joseph, and Robert Wicks. *Psychotherapy with Priests, Protestant Clergy and Catholic Vowed Religious*. Madison, CT: International Universities Press, 2000.

Coelho, Paulo. *The Alchemist*. New York: Harper, 2005.

Cousineau, Phil. *The Art of Pilgrimage*. Berkeley, CA: Conari Press, 1998.

Dalai Lama. *The Path to Tranquility*. Edited by Renuka Singh. New York: Viking, 1999.

de Mello, Anthony. *One Minute Wisdom*. New York: Doubleday, 1986.

Ellsberg, Robert. *The Saints' Guide to Happiness*. New York: Farrar, Straus, and Giroux, 2003.

Fischer, Norman. *Taking Our Places*. San Francisco: Harper, 2003.

Frankl, Viktor. *Man's Search for Meaning*. New York: Washington Square Press, 1963.

Hanh, Thich Nhat. *Essential Writing*. Maryknoll, NY: Orbis, 2001.

Henry, Patrick, ed. *Benedict's Dharma*. New York: Riverhead Books, 2001.

Heschel, Abraham. *The Wisdom of Heschel*. Edited by Ruth Marcus Goodhill. New York: Farrar, Straus, and Giroux, 1970.

Johnson, Sandy. *The Book of Tibetan Elders*. New York: Riverhead, 1996.

Johnston, William. *Christian Zen*. New York: Fordham, 1997.

Kabat-Zinn, Jon. *Wherever You Go, There You Are*. New York: Hyperion, 1994.

Kornfield, Jack. *After the Ecstasy, the Laundry*. New York: Bantam, 2000.

———. *A Path with Heart*. New York: Bantam, 1993.

Markides, Kyriacos. *Gifts of the Desert*. New York: Doubleday, 2005.

Maxwell, John. *Developing the Leader Within You*. Nashville: Thomas Nelson, 2005.

Merton, Thomas. *New Seeds of Contemplation*. New York: New Dimension, 1961.

———. *Thoughts in Solitude*. New York: Farrar, Straus, 1958.

Mother Teresa of Calcutta. *No Greater Love*. Novato, CA: New World Library, 1997.

Mott, Michael. *The Seven Mountains of Thomas Merton*. Boston: Houghton-Mifflin, 1984.

Nelson, Jack. *Hunger for Justice*. Maryknoll, NY: Orbis Press, 1980.

Norris, Kathleen. *Dakota*. Boston: Houghton-Mifflin, 1993.

Nouwen, Henri. *The Genesee Diary*. New York: Doubleday, 1976.

———. *Making All Things New*. San Francisco: Harper, 1981.

Paulsell, William. *Rules for Prayer*. Mahwah, NJ: Paulist, 1993.

Richardson, Robert D. *William James*. Boston: Houghton-Mifflin, 2006.

Rilke, Maria Ranier. *Book of Hours*. Translated by Anita Barrows and Joanna Macy. New York: Riverhead, 1996.

———. *Letters to a Young Poet*. New York: Norton, 1934.

Strand, Clark. *The Wooden Bowl*. New York: Hyperion, 1998.

Suzuki, Shunryu. *To Shine One Corner of the World*. Edited by David Chadwick. New York: Broadway, 2001.

Tolle, Eckardt. *The Power of Now*. San Rafael, CA: New World Library, 1999.

Ulmann, Liv. Quoted in: *The Wisdom of Women*. Edited by Carol Spenard La Russo. San Rafael, CA: New World Library, 1992.

Wicks, Robert. *Bounce: Living the Resilient Life*. New York: Oxford University Press, 2009.

———. *Crossing the Desert*. Notre Dame, IN: Sorin Books, 2007.

———. *Simple Changes*. Notre Dame, IN: Sorin Books, 2000.

———. *Touching the Holy*. Notre Dame, IN: Sorin Books, 1994.

ROBERT J. WICKS, who received his doctorate in psychology from Hahnemann Medical College, is on the faculty of Loyola University Maryland. Wicks has taught in universities and professional schools of psychology, medicine, social work, nursing, and theology. Wicks was responsible for the psychological debriefing of relief workers following the Rwandan civil war and also worked with relief teams in Cambodia. Additionally, he delivered presentations at Walter Reed Army Hospital to health-care professionals involved in caring for Iraqi war veterans with amputations and severe head injuries. He has authored over forty books, including *Riding the Dragon* and *Crossing the Desert*.

AVE

AVE MARIA PRESS

Founded in 1865, Ave Maria Press,
a ministry of the Congregation of
Holy Cross, is a Catholic publishing
company that serves the spiritual and
formative needs of the Church and its
schools, institutions, and ministers;
Christian individuals and families; and
others seeking spiritual nourishment.

For a complete listing of titles from

Ave Maria Press

Sorin Books

Forest of Peace

Christian Classics

visit www.avemariapress.com

AVE MARIA PRESS
Notre Dame, IN
A Ministry of the United States Province of Holy Cross